ATHENS
ATTICA

TOUBI'S ®

Text: Y. KOUKAS, ANNA MARANDI
Text Supervision: X. KAKAVOGIANIS
Photographs: D. KOLIOPANOU, T. SPYROPOULOS, Archives: M. TOUBIS S.A.

Artistic Supervision: NORA ANASTASOGLOU
.Typesetting, color separation, montage, printing: GRAPHIC ARTS M. TOUBIS S.A. - TEL. (01) 9923874

INTERNET: http://www.toubis.gr

CONTENTS

CONTENTS

Attica, where ancient Athens developed and achieved such great things, has come to mean a charismatic and unique site, a place that is blessed. And not by chance. Because the history of this region down through the centuries, and the achievements of the people who have lived there right up to the present are of inestimable value for the modern person, no matter where he or she might live.

And though the geographical position this place occupies was a positive factor in its amazing development, the perfecting of the arts, the probing into and promotion of the sciences and philosophy, and democracy itself, will always be seen as the offspring of the union of the Greek people with the soil of Attica, and a reflection of its spare beauty in Greek civilization. There is not one corner of Attica that does not have archaeological finds to bear witness to the passage of a people who built temples and founded settlements following the thread of local tradition.

The other end of this thread is lost in the Palaeolithic period, the dawn of mankind. The development of Attica, and above all its basin and coastline, gave birth to Athens. Athens, the city of intellect and light with a glorious history over 8,000 years old, the cradle of Greek civilization. In this corner of the European continent the human spirit bloomed and cast its fruits to Europe.

From its eternal flame the whole world would light a torch of devotion in order to illuminate the way to progress and the Renaissance, 2,000 years later.

"The Apotheosis of Homer"
a work by Ingres, in the Louvre.
The great epic poet is being crowned by Nike
in the presence of the great figures of history and the intellect.

e city of intellect and democracy

At a time when human beings had as yet not realized their true nature as beings, or their intrinsic worth, in order to resist the imposed authority of ancient societies, in Athens it was not just a chance experiment that was being carried out, but a true revolution of the human race, a social and spiritual springtime which liberated the Athenian citizen from all barriers to his creativity and natural abilities.

That is one reason why Athens had so many powerful enemies because anyone raised to maturity under the ideals of the Athenian state, and the Athenian culture, would not be able to abide any form of autocratic regime or authority; on the contrary, they would be eager to fight fiercely for their ideas.

Furthermore, this same people who was responsible for the great deeds at Marathon and Salamis, is still a model citizenry in its offering to and participation in public affairs and progress.

However, the unprecedented events that occurred long ago in that corner of the Mediterranean were not at all fortuitous. Nature itself favored Attica and endowed Athens in a way that the preconditions for an unprecedented event were created. The unique, deep blue sky, the pleasant climate, the sunshine and the clean air were the prerequisites for the people living in Athens to function with a penetrating mind and highly developed senses and to be distinguished as philosophers, poets, writers, orators and sculptors.

In a few words, all this is what gave ancient Athens its position in the world of that far-off time. Countless people linked their fate to the upward course of Athens. But the most important of them were the Athenians themselves, the children of the city, who according to Pericles, were obliged to lift it even higher. The town's form of government began to change in the 7th century B.C. with the reforms of Solon. Then the tyrants Peisistratos and Hipparchos (6th century) laid the foundations for Kleisthenis to found the Athenian Democracy, which was legislatively brought to perfection by Ephialtis and Pericles who carried on their work in the 5th century B.C.

This development was based on the growth of both philosophy and rhetoric which with the appearance of the Sophists also became a possession of the middle class.

Philosophers such as Socrates, Plato and the Sophists Hippias and Antiphon (who was the first to speak of the equality of all people) as well as Epicurus and, later, Aristotle raised

Greek thought to undreamed of heights. Together with them were the orators who spoke in public, and this gave the average citizen the chance to exercise his logical and dialectical abilities. This cultivation was also supplied by important historians such as Thucydides, the father of history as a science, and led to the development of the applied sciences.

Architecture, ship-building, astronomy, and the exploitation of metals (primarily at Lavrio) gave Athens the potential to dominate the Mediterranean with its ships, both economically and culturally.

Copperlate of Athens done in the middle of the 19th century.

Thus, Iktinos, Kallikratis and Mnisiklis would give to the world the gems that now adorn Athens: the Parthenon, the Propylaia and the other buildings on the rock of the Acropolis. The next step would be for the artists to fill the town with their works. Sculptors such as Myron, Phidias (whose works on the Parthenon were surpassed only by the statue of Olympian Zeus, which was also by him and one of the Seven Wonders of the Ancient World), and Alkamenis, Praxiteles, Leochares and Silanion, painters such as Nikias and musicians of the like of Damon and Lambroklis all helped to create a new aesthetic Parthenon of Art.

Ancient drama matured along with them and is still admired. Tragedy, founded by Thespis and Pratinas and with Aeschylus, Sophocles and Euripides as its leading representatives, continues to profoundly move us with the few remaining plays of the thousands that were written. But the comedy of Kratinos, Aristophanes and Menandros as well dealt with the same burning questions that have occupied man since the dawn of civilization, and were made with a humor and sensitivity that has seldom been equalled. But even so Athens cannot be easily explained as a phenomenon. The anonymous citizen must also be mentioned, the one who fought the Persian wars and went all the way to the Pillars of Hercules (Gibraltar), the citizen who for the first and perhaps the last time before the Renaissance, 2,000 years later, believed in his own value and abilities, in his own personality. The absence of a signature on the Sphinx or the Pyramids is replaced by "Kleitas created this". Athens won the respect of the rest of the world, because its citizens won the respect of their fellow man. Here we will insert several excerpts on the subject of civilization from the speech by the Frenchwoman Jacqueline de Romilly, a member of the French Academy and Honorary President of S.E.L. who was awarded the International Onassis Prize in 1995:

The superme work by Phidias,
the gold and ivory statue of Zeus on Mt. Olympus
and Athena Pallas on the Parthenon.

"...What happened here twenty five centuries ago had repercussions which can still be felt and their influence is of fundamental importance to our modern world. Here on the Pnyx is where the Assembly of the Deme was held. Here is where the heart of democracy beat. It was born in this town on the threshold of the 5th century B.C. And from its birth it reflected the pristine consciousness of the ancients which would be its very own form of eternity. The Greeks had understood by the time of the Medean Wars that their uniqueness lay in not bowing down to any man, in not accepting the absolute authority of any king. They had foreseen and proclaimed that the law was preferable to arbitrariness and justice to violence. That was proclaimed here, in the voice of such men as Themistocles and Pericles. And we have kept the brilliance of those bygone words, and they still move us today. Because the exceptional thing about Greece is not that it was the first to adopt a democratic regime. There could have been others.

Not even that it put into application a modern form of government. It's not that. It is rather that Greece was the first to define the beauty of such a regime and the preconditions for its application. Greeks also discerned, with time and experience, the dangers it contained and the mistakes to be avoided.

The phrases attributed to Pericles still echo here. It is not our origins in a given class but our ability that leads us to make distinctions. We apply the concept of freedom to all of our acts. "Ελευθέρως δε τα τε προς το κοινόν πολιτεύο-μεν...". Unforgettable words!

And here is also where in the following century Demosthenes censured the people most bitterly, imploring them to be more responsible, more effectual, and braver, because democracy, which was on the verge of collapse, demanded it ...
The democratic ideal, the ideal of justice, of tolerance and humanism, would perhaps not have come down to us if Greece had not imparted beauty to us. Demosthenes several times mentioned the view toward the Acropolis and the Propylaia.
Then he spoke with pride of the beauty of the monuments, the beauty of these ornaments . Furthermore Pericles proclaimed: "Φιλοκαλούμεν μετ'ευτελείας" (We love beauty that is unembellished).

"Pericles' speech from the Pnyx",
a work that was destroyed during the bombardement
of Athens by the Germans in World War II.

We have to admire a people who could conceive of this thought! But the meaning of the beautiful in ancient Greece was not only related to sculpture or architecture. The true creation, poetry, aimed at the beautiful and thereby sought to achieve the permanent. The writers who did not write beautifully have been forgotten: we no longer have the discussions of the Sophists, the obscure historians and the unsuccessful poets. We have the great literary works which are able to take a great idea or emotion and send it straight to the heart of the reader or the audience. In our modern world which is full of clumsily written articles, and files in an incomprehensible language, ancient Greek writing comes as a relief.

The meaning of the beautiful is closely connected to the meaning of the ideal and the presence of this trust in man. And this is what we need today. A little enthusiasm for democratic principles would do us good, not to mention a little zest for life and a little more valor all of which can be found in these texts and which, because of the way they are expressed, are still living, vibrant, ready to create anew...
"..If we defend the presence of ancient Greek principles in our modern education we do not do it because it belongs to the past of all of us, but because it is the best guarantee for the future...".

NATURE

Athens in the Attica basin

Looking for Attica on the map of Greece you will find its triangular geophysical relief spreading out into the western Aegean. It is the southernmost point of mainland Greece and is washed by the Euboean, Saronic and Corinthian Gulfs. The peninsula ends to the south at Cape Sounion where are found the ruins of the temple of Poseidon. The unique position of Attica in the Eastern Mediterranean basin has made it necessary since ancient times to have a large harbor there, such as the Athenians had at Piraeus, which is still the largest one in the country and which facilitates communications in the area. The position of Athens in the basin is defined by Mt. Parnitha and Mt. Penteli whose great masses command the north. Mt Hymettus dominates the east while to the west are the numerous low hills of Aegaleio and Korydallos. Penteli has been renowned since antiquity for its superb marble, the raw material used by sculptors and the basic construction material for the monuments of Attica, where Hymettus is known for its pure thyme-flavored honey. There are also hills in the middle of the basin. These include Tourkovounia (335 m.); Lycabettus (277 m.), which according to many still has a pre Greek name (as does Hymettus: the "ttus" ending), with the white chapel of St. George at its summit and its theatre bearing the same name; Ardittus (133 m.) which lies above the stadium and is there the judges of the Helliaia took their oath during antiquity; Philopappou hill (147 m.); the hill of the Nymphs (104 m.) where the planetarium is located above the picturesque Theseio temple the Pynx hill (109 m.) and other smaller ones. Among all of these is the one that glorified not only Athens but the whole Greek world and became the heart of the ancient world: the rock of the Acropolis! Athens has developed and spread out in this basin to the point that it has become one with the port of Piraeus while the suburbs have spilled outside the basin itself.

The morphology of the land is characterized by a constant alteration between low mountains and small plains. To the north is Mt. Kithaironas (1,404 m.) and the verdant Parnitha (1,413 m.) while Penteli (1,109 m.) lies in the center. The top of the arc is completed to the west by the low, rocky hill of Aigaleo and Hymettus to the east (1,206 m.). The picturesque peculiarities of the Attic coast make it look like a long piece of lace. According to one theory, it owes its name to these coasts ("Attiki", "Aktiki" coming from "Akti" which means coast). Bays and small rocky or sandy coves dot the area and during the summer are filled with locals and foreigners enjoying their beauty. Outside the Attica peninsula, but still in the Prefecture of Attica, are the islands of Aegina, Salamis, Hydra, Poros, Kithera and the area of Troizina. The river system of Athens is of no particular interest. There are two streams, the Kifissos and the Ilissos which since ancient times have collected the rainwater that fell on the basin and directed it to their mouths in the bay of Phaliro. Of the plains it is worth mentioning those of Eleusis and Athens, the Mesogeia in partcular, which is fertile and systematically cultivated. The topographic conditions we have mentioned keep the climate of Athens from being a marine one, as would be expected from the marked presence of the sea all around, but temperate and very healthy.

--- The boundaries of the borders of Attica

Archaeological sites

Caves

Monasteries

Airport

The four seasons all have their own definite
characteristics and are perceptibly different
as one succeeds the other. Spring is relatively
short, usually confined to March, and is quite
chilly, growing quickly milder in April and May.
That means summer begins early and is hot,
the driest month being July while the first
autumn rains appear in September.
Winter begins in December when most
of the rain falls and reaches its peak in the cold
days of January but it also has a mild period
known as the Halcyon days.
According to Greek tradition, Halcyon, the lover
of Zeus, was changed by the god into a bird to
save her from the rage of Hera. These mild
days, when Halcyon hatched her eggs, were
Zeus' gift to his lover. Attica has always been
generous to its inhabitants. Its land produces
agricultural and garden products, olives from
the tree that the goddess Athena gave to the
town of Athens, grapes and the famed wine
from the vineyards in the area, such as the
retsina from the Mesogeia. There are also the
thyme honey, the natural resin of the pine trees,
the salt and the fish; these are but a few of the
gifts which Attica gives us not to mention
pentelic marble and the silver that was formerly
extracted from the mines at Lavrio.
The sunshine of Attica and its pleasant climate
give the host of visitors to Greece the
opportunity to enjoy it during all seasons.
Besides a planned program of visits to specific
places, one always has the opportunity to get
away to the countryside, to the mountains or
the sea. The distances are not far and the
changes in the weather, even in winter,
hold pleasant surprises in store: a heavy rain
is often followed by brilliant sunshine!

*Attica has a rich history with
a very influential tradition of intellectual creativity,
but it also has fertile land and a munificent sea.*

3

MYTH & HISTORY

Mythology - The Golden Age
The Roman & Byzantine periods - Modern times

The political and cultural development that was a hallmark of Attica, with its center at Athens, was due to its being an enclosed geographical unit and the fact that its indigenous inhabitants had a common origin. The beginning of the history of Athens is lost in the darkness of time. But what history ignores is filled in by myth and tradition at least in what concerns the gods who had a direct relationship with the town of Athens, through their clashes over which of them would be its protector, whether to accept the gifts of Poseidon, Athena and Dionysos. Myth even speaks about the great mythical men of the town such as Kekrops and Theseus. If the Athenians had been named for their heroic founder they would have been called Kekropidans. Kekrops was half serpent and half man and spawned by the earth.

Pensive Athena, 460 B.C.
(Akropolis Museum, room 6).

The Athenians stated that their first king, Kekrops, instituted monogamy and the burial of the dead. He also took part in the Council of the Twelve Gods of Olympus when Poseidon, the god of the sea, and Athena, the goddess of wisdom, were laying claim to Attica. According to myth, when the time came for their showdown, Poseidon struck the rock of the Acropolis with his trident and at that point a horse sprang out and rushing water. Athena replied by striking the rock right next to it with her spear and the first olive tree sprang forth. The gods finally declared Athena the victor and thus she became the protectress of the town which took her name. In order to placate Poseidon the Athenians dedicated an impressive temple to him at the southeastern edge of Attica, at Sounion.

Attica also has connections to two other divinities: Dionysos the god of wine and intoxication. The vineyard was the gift of this god to his be-loved city of Athens. Attica celebrated the Dionysia, an uninhibited festival, in his honor with dances and processions. Tragedy and comedy were born of the dithyrambic performances which were given during the ceremonies. Attica is also connected to the goddes Demeter and her daughter Persephone whom Hades abducted as his wife. During the goddess' despairing quest for her daughter she was given hospitality at the home of Keleos, the King of Eleusis. In gratitude for the hospitality he had offered her, she taught the inhabitants of Eleusis how to cultivate the earth, and the Eleusinian Mysteries. At the site where they first encountered the goddess, the temple was built in which the Eleusinian Mysteries were conducted.

Terracotta mask used in ancient drama.

Dionysos and Ariadne, bronze krater.

Before the appearance of the Greeks, Athens was inhabited by the Pelasgians (3rd millennium B.C.).

The oldest walls of the Acropolis, today called the Pelasgian or Cyclopean walls, are credited to them, as well as many of the ancient temples, and the names of rivers and mountains in Attica such as Hymettus, Lycabettus and so on.

In the middle of the second millennium the Ionians settled in Attica (their name derives from their mythical ancestor Ionas).

After their settlement, Attica was divided into separate small towns which made their own, independent decisions and only held consultations with the king in times of war. Then Kekrops appeared, and he is considered to be the first king of Athens. His successors were Pandion, Erecheus, Aegeus and finally, Theseus.

These were all fabled kings and they made a great contribution to the progress and development of the city.

The myth, however, sheds particular light on Theseus, the demigod hero of Athens who accomplished amazing feats with his incredible physical strength and his free spirit.

During his journey to Athens, to succeed his father Aegeus, Theseus was put to six tests, three of which took place in Attica. He dealt with Sciron in the Megarid, in the area that is still called the Scironian Rocks, Cercyon in Eleusis and Procrustes on Mt. Korydallos.

But the greatest feat of Theseus was the liberation of Athens from the yearly tribute of 7 young men and 7 maidens who were sent to the Ruler of the Seas, Minos, King of Crete, as victims for the Minotaur. Theseus was also Hercules' escort in his labor against the Amazons.

His glory was so great he ended being considered the founder of Athens.

To him is attributed the act of uniting the small settlements of the area and the creation of a single town, Athens.

This act was celebrated with great processions and contests called the Panathenaia.

Theseus is said to have been the first to bring democracy to the kingdom, founding a Senate and Prytaneum.

Athens before the 5th century

The Descent of the Dorians in the 12th century B.C. brought an end to the Mycenean civilization in southern Greece. When later the Dorians invaded Attica, in 1066 B.C., the Athenians went against them under King Kodros, who fell heroically on the field of battle. During that period the population was divided into four races and the body of the citizenry into three classes: the Eupatrides (Patricians nobles and landowners) the farmers and the artisans. At the beginning of the 8th century B.C. power passed to these Eupatrides and the king retained only the direction of the official sacrifices. The military command acquired a chief who was named for life, the executive authority was assumed by an Archon and the enactment of laws by a group of legislators. With the gradual decline of the monarchy, an aristocratic regime was established by the nobles and landowners who held authority in their hands. In the middle of the 7th century B.C. there were a large number of social and political disturbances in Athens. In 594 B.C. Solon drafted legislation that organized the state on the basis of the citizens' income. This state, based on "worth" (a timocracy), even though it was the first stage of democracy, did not get rid of social conflict. This was resolved by a "tyranny", that is, the assumption of power by an absolute ruler.

The Tyrant, usually an aristocrat, sought to insure popular support with the ceding of land and the carrying out of public works. One of the main factors in Athen's course toward democracy was the tyrant Peisistratos who ruled the city during the 6th century B.C. His concern for the arts and sciences created a cultural explosion, which was socially effective. His policies also led to a vast increase of the output of the mines at Lavrio in the 5th century B.C. as well as the rapid growth of the town's commerce.
But the contribution of Peisistratos to the development of the religious and cultural life of the town is also considered significant: he imbued the worship of Athena, the protectress of the town, with particular brilliance, building her Hecatopedon and enhancing the Panathenaia. He facilitated the spread of the Eleusinian Mysteries and established the Dionysia, thus contributing to the creation of tragedy and comedy.
To him is also attributed the writing down of the Homeric epics. With the fall of the Peisistratid line, equilibrium was brought to Athenian society by the great politician Kleisthenis in 508 B.C. His reforms gave the Athenian citizens institutions to consolidate the power that would stop the extension of the Persian Empire onto the European continent on land and sea .

The 5th century B.C.
The Golden Age of Pericles

At the beginning of the 5th century B.C. the Persians decided on a campaign against the Greeks, spurred mainly by the uprising of the Greeks in Ionia (the coast of Asia Minor). The conquest of the Greek peninsula and the Aegean Sea, however, would be stopped with their annihilation in 490 B.C. at Marathon. Athens, led in this battle by Miltiadis, showed its superiority over the rest of the Greeks. The Persians took their defeat hard and ten years later lead by Xerxes, the successor to the Persian throne, they again got as far as Attica, but were once more defeated by the Athenians, this time at the naval battle of Salamis (480 B.C.). The leading role in this victory was yet again played by Athens led by Themistocles and his advisor Aristidis the Just. A year later the triumph of the Greeks over the Persians was sealed once and for all at the battle of Plataies with the Athenian victory. This was the clash of two worlds. Proud, vibrant with passion and possessed of strong individuality, the Greeks had the vitality which permitted them to triumph over the superior forces of the absolutist Persians. Until then Sparta had been leader of the Greek city-states. But the Persian Wars brought a new power to the fore, Athens. The assumption of power by Pericles was a catalytic element for the deme as he himself eloquently described it in his Funeral Oration of Thucydides. The Athenians were endowed with such a forceful character that it set them apart from other Greeks.

They confronted the problems of existence with dynamism and an innovative spirit which constituted the clearest expression of Hellenism both on a spiritual and political level and had a direct influence on the entire new Western world.

The threat of civil strife between Athens and the other great power, Sparta, had begun to grow and would mark the 5th century B.C. irredeemably. Themistocles had foreseen this danger and done everything he could to avoid it. He made the walls of Athens impregnable, constructed the harbor at Piraeus and made the sea power of the town even stronger. Kimon carried on the work of Themistocles and with his victories at the Eurymedon River (466 B.C.), Thasos, the Hellespont and elsewhere, drove the Persians completely out of the Mediterranean and made the Aegean Sea Greek. The Athenian Alliance of 478 B.C. united all the islands and the coastal areas of the Aegean. Kimon beautified Athens with works and transformed the Academy at Kolonos into a paradise of amusement for the Athenians. During the time of Kimon, Aeschylus (472 B.C.) put on his "Persians" at the Theatre of Dionysos. The choragos (producer) of this performance was Pericles who made his first public appearance in this way. After the death of Kimon the Assembly of the people needed an enlightened leader and found it in the person of Pericles. A young landowner who came from a large family he had a wide-ranging intellect, a superb education and a moving eloquence.

He reformed many of the laws of Solon, strengthened democracy, the army and the fleet, increased the wages of the judges, established free theater for the people and under his guidance Athens reached its zenith. During the 50 years 479-431 B.C. which would follow the end of the Persian wars, Athenian **Democracy** would be completed with the reforms of **Pericles.** The achievements in the arts and letters were owed to the equality under the law of all citizens The contribution of Athens to the cultural and political sector constituted the basis of European civilization.

Kiln for the refining of ore.
The silver and lead from the mines
at Lavrio provided the economic support
for the Golden Age of Athens.

Bust of Pericles.

Bust of Socrates.

Pericles. *The man who made Athenian Democracy a worldwide symbol, the man who gave his name to an entire century, is characterized by Schackermeyr as the political embodiment of the perfect classical style that occurred for the first time in human history.*

A charismatic man, he ruled the most inspired but also the most difficult regime in history because every citizen was a conscious member of the whole society.

Democracy means the "state of the deme", that is, the assembly of the people makes the decisions.

The fact that Pericles shone in such a brilliant state exalts him even more. The phrase "the Golden Age of Pericles" summarizes the work of this great leader with an incorruptible character, with a well-directed and consistent policy which saw not only to political development but spiritual growth as well.

Pericles and the sculptor Phidias. *A coexistence that produced miracles. The aim of Pericles was to make Athens the "Greece within Greece". His primary concern was the beautification of the sacred rock of the Acropolis. His first work the Parthenon.*

This was followed by the Erechtheion, the Theseion and the Propylaia.
And a little further away the temples of Poseidon at Sounion, Nemesis at Rhamnous, and Aris at Acharnes.
Phidias - Iktionos - Kallikratis and Mnisiklis their works are still admired.

The Athens of Pericles, *the greatest miracle in the history of the world, attracted looks of both admiration and hostility.*
The cold war with Sparta.was halting in the beginning but became threatening later. Catastrophe loomed on the horizon by 431 B.C. The civil war broke out and it would set the fate of Greece. The tragic nature and the brutality of this war would be set forth by the greatest historian of antiquity, Thucydides. After an endless series of successes and failures the fate of Athens was decided at sea. In August 405 B.C. the Spartan admiral Lysandros captured most of its fleet's triremes. Finally, in April 404 B.C. Athens was forced to capitulate. Lysandros immediately tore down the Long Wall and the walls around Piraeus. After the end of the war power was handed over to thirty oligarchs.

They ruled so harshly for 8 months that the period is still known as the time of the Thirty Tyrants. In 403 B.C. Thrasyvoulos brought back a democratic regime. A new period began for Athens but one also marred by the sentencing to death of Socrates in 399 B.C.

The 4th century B.C.
The Macedonians

Some of the greatest artists, orators, philosophers, politicians and generals appeared in the 4th century B.C. This was the age of Plato, Xenophon, Praxiteles, Demosthenes and Lykourgos. The Pnyx became the altar of democracy, Plato founded his Academy, Aristotle elevated Greek philosophy to the absolute and Athens reclaimed its rule of the sea. But this was only a brief revival since Athens defeat at Chaironeia (338 B.C.) marked the definitive end of the city-states of antiquity.

"The Death of Socrates",
a work by David from the 18th century.

That was when the Macedonian Sun appeared. Demosthenes launched rhetorical attacks against it but in the end it conquered the state of Athens.
Demosthenes then drank hemlock in the temple of Poseidon on Poros so he would not be handed over flo the Macedonians, the first people who managed to unite all Greeks under their rule.
Soon after, Alexander the Great honored Athens and sent the shields from his victory at the Granikos River to be placed in the Parthenon.
During the period of the Successors of Alexander the Great, Athens was constantly gaining and losing its independence.
Despite its collapse Athens again was a gathering point for the wisdom of the scientists, the artists and the educators.
The kings of Pergamon and Ptolemaic Egypt decked out the former city of light in order to show their devotion. But the constant civil disputes gave a new global power, Rome, the excuse to intervene in Greece.

The Roman period

The Romans dissolved the Macedonian state in 146 B.C. and occupied Athens, but in a lenient and apparently friendly way. Then the great plunder began.

Thousands of statues and other works of art were transported from Athens to Rome. In 86 B.C. the harsh and inhuman Roman Sylla cut down all the trees in the Academy during his siege of Athens, pulled down the walls and the shipyards of Piraeus, bombarded the Odeon of Pericles and plundered the treasury of the Parthenon.

But despite its military and political enfeeblement, Athens continued to be the center of the arts and sciences. During the period of the emperors, Augustus, Agrippa, Nero and Hadrian the Temple of Olympian Zeus, Hadrian's Gate, and the Roman Aqueduct were built. Herod Atticus built the Herodeon Theater and renovated the Stadium.

Marcus Aurelius encouraged the philosophical schools of Athens. During the period of Roman rule the Theater of Dionysos was transformed into an arena for fights with wild beasts and gladiators, the victims being the first Athenian Christian martyrs.

The town's condition was described by Pausanias in the middle of the 2nd century A.D. and shortly thereafter the orator Aristidis called it the most beautiful of cities.

In 267 and 395 A.D. the Heruli and the Goths under Alaric successively devastated the city and its environs. From then until the split of the Roman Empire (the birth of Byzantium) into east and west, Athens would occupy a secondary position in the Roman world.

Byzantine times

But the ancient spirit did not find fertile ground to develop despite the desperate efforts of the Greek-nurtured emperor Julian.
The destruction of the ancient monuments in a number of cases, would be taken as examples of the faith of the converts.
The final blow would be given the town in 529 with the closing of the philosophical schools by Justinian.
By the end of the 4th century A.D. the antiquities were deserted and many were in ruins. The Athenian empress of Byzantium Evdokia (408-450) did build various buildings in her place of birth. But the city did not play any real role in the life of the empire.

Hadrian's Gate,
a Roman monument that lies in the center of Athens.

The construction of churches in Athens and the transformation of ancient temples into Christian churches began in the middle of the 5th century. The Parthenon became the church of the Panayia Atheniotissa (The Virgin Mary the Athenian) the church of Ayioi Anargyroi (Sts. Kosmas and Daimion) was built in the Asclepeion, a small church was erected in the Theater of Dionysos and two large triple-aisled churches were built in the Temple of Olympian Zeus. From the 7th to the 9th century, the history of Athens is shrouded in deep darkness. Epidemics, earthquakes, and the invasions of hostile peoples left it deserted. The Bulgarians had reached Attica. In 1018 the emperor Basil II drove out the Bulgarians and in 1019 he came as a pilgrim to the Panayia Atheniotissa on the Acropolis. Despite the continued incursions of the Bulgarians and the Normans, the Byzantine aristocrat Nikolaos Kalomalos built Ayioi Theodoroi in Athens and a collector of tobacco tax built Kapnikarea church.

Athens was slowly filled with Byzantine churches. (See chapter "Byzantine Athens", p. 96). Until then the city still was in fairly good condition and had a very powerful defense because of its three successive enclosures. The destruction of the town which is referred to in the ballad "Lament for Athens" must have occurred at the end of the 12th century and can be attributed to Saracen pirates. From 1182 until the seizure of the town by the Franks in 1204 the Metropolitan of Athens was Michael Choniatis. In his speeches and writings he paints a grievous picture of the misery the city was experiencing after the plague but above all the destruction it had suffered from the pirate raids.

The Temple of Hephaestus (Theseion), the best preserved temple from the time of Pericles, found in the Ancient Agora.

The Franks - The Turkish occupation

In the 13th century Athens surrendered to the Franks after Constantinople fell to them (1204). It was ruled by the dukes de la Roche who built their tower in the Propylaia of the Acropolis. The period of the 4th Crusades marked a new beginning and Attica was to experience the medieval western mentality for two and a half centuries. During the time of the Renaissance the West would seek out the sleeping spirit of the town. Plato and Aristotle declared peaceful coexistence with Christian idealism. In Athens, however, the Turks would succeed the Venetians in 1456 and would be entranced by the ancient monuments. Thus they would transform the Parthenon into a mosque and the Erechtheion into a harem! Up until the 19th century our only information on the town is from the descriptions of travellers who came from European countries to see this once glorious city. Many of them returned to their homeland bearing souvenirs of their trip: statues, amphoras and whatever else could be transported. European museums and private collections are full of these souvenirs. The first serious damage as well as the first bleeding away of antiquities occurred through the emissary sent by the West to assist the enslaved Christian Greeks, the Venetian **Morosini**. Arriving in Athens this Commander-in-Chief found the Turks shut up inside the Acropolis where they had transformed the Parthenon into a temporary powder storehouse. During his siege of the Sacred Rock he bombarded the ancient monument, causing incalculable damage. The Parthenon which had become a powder magazine for the Turks was blown up by the bombardment. The campaign failed and when he left Morosini took three marble lions with him. Two of these (the lion that was at the harbor of Piraeus and the one at the Theseio) are today at the entrance to the naval station of Venice. But the greatest looting of antiquities was done by the English ambassador to Constantinople Lord Elgin, who plundered the Parthenon, the Acropolis and many other archaeological sites destroying many sculptures of incalculable value.

More recent times

In 1821 the Greek struggle for liberation began. The country became independent and in 1834 King Othon came to the new capital of the Greek state, Athens. During the same year the Acropolis ceased to be used as a fortress and was deemed an archaeological monument and the work for its cleaning and repair were begun. In 1896 the first modern Olympics were held, a cosmopolitan pause in the disturbed course of the country. Slowly this small market town would begin to reacquire its lost glory and beauty. Public buildings and villas, influenced by western European neoclassical architecture, with enormous gardens, made up the bulk of the city which occupied only the historic center of Athens. Among the buildings two stood out: the palace of the King (the present Parliament) in the National Garden and the Old Parliament today a museum.

Copperplate of Athens from the beginning of the 20th century.

Stamp commemorating the revival of the Olympic Games.

Below the Sacred Rock the poor houses of the craftsmen who came to build the capital cling to the hill; this was **Plaka** which later would become a complete settlement on its own and be called the "neighborhood of the Gods".
Kleanthis - Schaubert - Ziller. Three names that set their mark on the creation of this town with their architectural masterpieces.
After World War I and the Asia Minor Disaster in 1922 a serious housing problem was created because of the large influx of refugees into Athens.

But the worst time the capital experienced was during World War II.
After the war the town endeavored to stand on its own two feet again. With the destruction of its productive forces, poverty and unemployment came to the foreground. But its citizens were not intimidated and carried on, as always with the same indomitable optimism and faith in their own powers.
The German occupation and the Greek resistance led to the desertion of the countryside.
This caused a great wave of urbanization. The full-scale rebuilding of the capital, which now has nearly half the population of Greece concentrated in it, brought with it the problems of all large cities. Athens changed, but the visitor can still find many exciting things.
The representation of all the periods of Greek history in one place is bound to arouse the visitor's interest.

4

THE ACROPOLIS

History - Monuments - The Parthenon
The Museum - On the slopes of the sacred Rock

The rock of the Acropolis rises up in the middle of the Athenian basin, 156 m. above sea level, with a length of 300 m. and a width of 150 m. Its position is of particular strategic importance because of the view it affords of all the surrounding a-

Reproduction of the temple and the other buildings on the Acropolis.

rea, and down to the sea. This is the reason it was inhabited even during the prehistoric period. The Pelasgians, the first inhabitants of Athens, fortified this rock with walls made of enormous slabs 6 m. wide. These were the Cyclopean or Pelasgian walls. The cyclopean walls protected the king's palace and the houses of his officers. During the early historical period a temple dedicated to Poseidon, the god of the sea, and Athena, the goddess of wisdom, was erected on the site of the old palace. The temple was destroyed twice and rebuilt both times. In the 6th century B.C. it was decorated with marvellous works of sculpture.

Pausanias informs us about the forms of religious worship that developed on the north side of the sacred rock. On the northwest side the remains of a spring have survived which after the Medean Wars was fashioned into a building

for a fountain. It is known as the **Klepsydra** and had been used for a water supply since prehistoric times. In front of the Klepsydra was the intersection of the Panathenaic Way and the **Peripatos** (The Promenade) The Peripatos went a-

round the Acropolis passing along the slopes of the rock and reaching the Herod Atticus Odeon. To the east of the Klepsydra were three caves which have been identified as the **sanctuaries of Apollo, Pan** and the **Olympian Zeus**. Even further down was a staircase that led to the sanctuary dedicated to **Aglauro**, one of the daughters of Kekrops. According to Pausanias a path that started there led to an area that was dedicated to the worship of **Aphrodite tis en Kirois** (Aphrodite in the Gardens) and **Eros**. After the establishment of the Panathenaia the **Propylaia** were built on the west end of the rock along with the **Temple of Athena Nike**. Many other temples were built on the Acropolis dedicated both to the gods and to demigods, heroes and evil spirits. In 480 B.C. the Acropolis as well as the rest of Athens was burned and reduced to ruins by the Persian army.

The Monuments on the Acropolis

The monuments we see today are works from the Classical period. It is thought that they were erected by Pericles during the period 447-406 B.C. and reflect a single plan.

The artistic staff that was employed includes the names of the architects Iktinos, Mnisiklis and Kallikrates.

There is also Phidias who was a sculptor but had far greater influence. In brief, the monuments of the Acropolis contain the most representative examples of the astonishing Attican architecture of the Classical period.

The Beulé Gate

The **Beulé** Gate has two towers, one of which, rebuilt in modern times, is used for issuing entrance tickets to the Acropolis. It took its name from the French archaeologist **Ernest Beulé** who did the excavations in this area in 1852. This is one of the two gates in the fortified walls which were constructed after the invasion of the Herouli in 267 A.D.

The Sanctuary of Pandimos Aphrodite

Right of the **Beulé** gate are the remains of the temple of Aphrodite. Today a section of the temple's architrave still survives, decorated with garlands and doves.

Agrippa's Plinth

In front of the north wing of the Propylaia can be seen the remains of a high plinth. This pedestal was built in the first half of the 2nd century B.C. as a base for a quadriga, a votive offering by Eumenis II, King of Pergamon, after his victory in the Panathenaic Games in 178 B.C.

Later, in 27 B.C., the same pedestal held the dedication of the Athenians to Marcus Agrippa in honor of his beneficent works for the town.

The Propylaia

The Propylaia, which were never completed, were built between 437-432 B.C. on the plans of the architect Mnisiklis and pentelic marble and Eleusinian stone were used in their construction. This was an imposing structure that was erected on the site of the old Propylon, based on plans that were very advanced, both from an architectural and artistic point of view. The entire structure was made up of a central rectangular space of large dimensions, amphiprostyle with six Doric columns on the east (interior) side and the west (exterior) side.

Above: Model of the Acropolis during the Roman period.

Below: Plan of the Monuments on the Acrropolis.

1. Entrance
2. Klepsydra Fountain
3. Agrippa Monument
4. Gallery
5. Propylaia
6. Temple of Athena Nike
7. Temple of Artemis Brauvronia
8. Chalkotheke
9. Parthenon
10. Temple of Rome and Augustus
11. Museum
12. Temple of Aphrodite Pandemos
13. Temple of Zeus Polieos
14. Altar of Athena
15. "Ancient Temple" of Athena
16. Pandroseion
17. Erechtheion
18. Arrephoreion
19. Statue of Athena Promachus
20. Promenades
21. Street of the Panathenaia
22. The Herod Atticus Theater
23. Eumenos Stoa
24. Asclepieion
25. Choregic Monument of Nikia
26. Choregic Monument of Thrasyllos
27. The Theater of Dionysos
28. The Odeon of Pericles

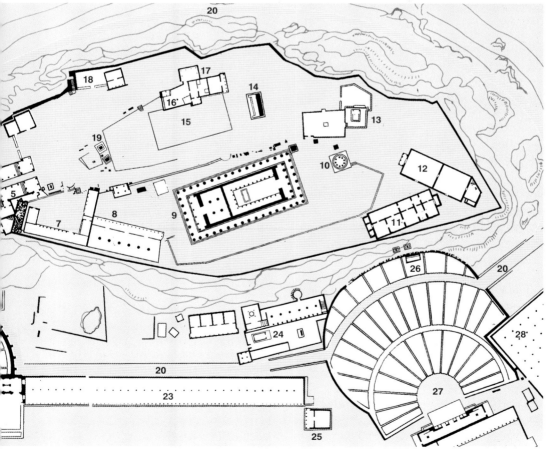

This main section was to be framed by four large halls arranged symmetrically by twos.

Two Ionic colonnades were placed in its interior, at right angles to the colonnade of the facade, for the support of the roof which thus created three aisles, the narrowest in the middle. The eastern part of the structure, following the natural formation of the land, was built at a higher level.

The communication between the eastern and western areas was accomplished by five successive entrances closed by heavy wooden doors. The difference in height was dealt with by the use of a separate roof.

Of the four chambers in the two wings of the Propylaia only the one on the north wing of the west side was fully completed. It was pillared with three Doric columns set between pilasters and the entrance openings were deliberately symmetrical. Left and right were windows placed at irregular intervals. Originally it must have been used as a place for visitors to wait and rest with couches placed around its circumference. It is known as the "Art Gallery" because according to Pausanias it was used for the exhibition of paintings.

In the south wing, and corresponding to the Gallery, there was another small room whose construction was dictated by reasons of aesthetics and the harmony of the whole. It was also pillared with three Doric columns between the pilasters which together with those opposite them (in the Gallery) formed an enclosed reception space which was used as the main entrance. But this room, oddly enough, was never completed, probably for reasons of religious expediency.

Its extension further south would have meant the blocking off of parts of the Mycenean Pelasgian walls as well as the tower with the temple of the Wingless Nike.

The Athenian Propylaia were not completed because of the Peloponnesian wars which broke out in 431 B.C. But the faultless morphological solutions that were found and the relationships of the proportions used in Mnisiklis design made for one of the most important monuments.

The Temple of Athena Nike

This is a small, elegant Ionian monument built on a bastion on the southwest side of the rock of the Acropolis. The temple must have been built between 427-424 B.C. and Kallikrates is mentioned as its architect. Excavations have brought to light, on the same site, building elements from the Mycenean period. That is when the powerful bastion must have been built. Later, during Archaic times, that is, during the period of the Peisistratids, a very small temple was erected on the Mycenean fortification, dedicated to the worship of Athena. The Persians destroyed them in 480 B.C., but the space was included in Pericles' building program and later the bastion was completed and dressed with poros limestone thus becoming the tower we see today.

The Ionian temple, made entirely of pentelic marble which was erected on a podium, magnifies the unaffected grandeur of the sacred rock and gives a different spirit to the entire cluster of monuments.

It is a monument of small dimensions, amphiprostyle and four-pillared. It has monolithic columns with relatively low proportions and high bases with a large scotia. The eastern side of the nave was divided into pilasters and two pillars and the openings were enclosed with railings.

The religious statue of the Nike, with its cut-off wings, was housed in the nave, which was fashioned into a crypt by three steps.

That is why Pausanias said in the 2nd century A.D. that the temple was dedicated to the Wingless Victory (Nike = Victory).

The sculptural decoration of the monument was of particular note. The frieze that went round the temple on all four sides depicted the following subjects: on the east side there was the assembly of the Gods of Olympus with Zeus and Poseidon on either side of Athena and on the other sides were depicted battles of the Greeks against the Barbarians and Greeks against Boeotians.

The built-in sculptures as well as the gilded bronze acrotiria have been lost.

The temple of the Wingless Nike, a symbol of the faith of the Athenians in their political system.

Around 410 B.C. the tower was enclosed with a parapet on the top on the south, west and north sides. The marble plaques of the parapet are of great artistic value containing exceptional bas-reliefs which depict Nikes and a repetition of the image of the seated Athena.

Important fragments of these marble plaques have survived. Both the figures on the frieze and the figures on the parapet are superb examples of the mature so-called "rich" style.

The Temple of Brauronian Artemis

The temple, which is found on a site east of the remainders of the Mycenean walls, was fashioned with a Doric portico and two projecting wings in a "u" shape with a peribolos.

Its founding is attributed to the tyrant Peisistratos who came from the district of Brauron where the worship of Artemis was particularly widespread. In the wings off the portico were housed the two statues of the goddess: the first, an Archaic wooden statue, showed the goddess enthroned and the second, as Pausanias mentioned, was the work of the sculptor Praxiteles. Both of the wings must have functioned as Treasuries and the outdoor part of the temple was full of votive offerings. Around the 4th century B.C. a second portico was added in front of the east wing of the already existing one.

Today only a few remains of the foundations and carvings on the rock have survived.

Chalkothiki

The inscriptions explain the name of this edifice, which lies east of the Brauronia. This was the Chalkothiki whose purpose was to house and protect the metal offerings which belonged to the goddess Athena. It was built in the middle of the 5th century B.C. and at the beginning of the 4th century B.C. it was enlarged with a porch. The discovery of various architectural members testify to repair done to the building during the Roman period.

45

The Parthenon

During the period 495-480 B.C. the Athenians began to build, on the site of the present-day Parthenon, a marble six-columned Doric temple which was never completed. Its sterobate and its foundation and a section of its upper structure were later incorporated by Pericles into the Parthenon. After the destruction of this half completed work, by the Persians, in 480 B.C. the Athenians abandoned the idea of rebuilding the temple, until Pericles appeared in the political arena and promoted the grandeur of Athens

This grand building program was most obviously concerned with the projection of the Athenian state, of the vision that was realized by Athenian democracy, and of the glory and the prestige the town had acquired after the Persian wars. So at the highest point of the Sacred Rock the Athenians erected one of the most perfect creations of the human spirit, a symbol of classical beauty and perhaps the supreme achievement of ancient Greek architecture. Both the conception of the idea of the Parthenon and its execution gave the building an a uniqueness all its own.

The erection began in 447 B.C. and the
inauguration was held in 438 B.C. during
the celebration of the Panathenaic Games.
The sculptural decoration of the building
would be completed in 432 B.C. Iktinos and
Kallikratis are known as the architects of the
Parthenon. Unfortunately, it is not known what
each of them did and even if they worked
together or one succeeded the other.
In any case, the decoration program
and the general supervision of the structural
work was handled by Phidias.

"Phidias and the Frieze of the Parthenon", Sir Lawrence Alm-Tadema, 1866, Athens.

The temple is Doric, peripteral, with eight columns on each facade and 17 columns on the long sides and with general dimensions at the level of the stylobate of 30.86 x 69.51 m. Its nave, amphiprostyle and with six columns, was divided into two unequal parts.

Of those, the one to the east was a two-storeyed Doric porch in a "u" shape which housed the religious statue of Athena, while the smaller western one had a more or less square plan, four Ionic columns to support the roof and was accessible only from the opisthodromos. From the beginning this part was called the Parthenon. There have been various theories formulated regarding its function; the most prevalent one is that it was used as the town's treasury.

The entire temple was made of pentelic marble except for the wooden roof and the poros limestone foundation. It is distinguished for its astonishing technical perfection which graces the building with a completely original harmony. The curves of the horizontal and vertical surfaces of the temple were not, of course, employed here for the first time, but were already known in Archaic times.

However, in the Parthenon they achieve their most perfect form. Here are found all the so-called visual corrections and refinements of the Doric style, in a system so strictly adhering to set proportions that nothing could have resulted but a perfectly balanced and harmonious whole. The conscious lack of straight lines lends charm and vitality to the building, and lightens the mass, breathing life into the monument.

The ambitious morphological intentions of the planners can be seen in a series of innovations to the building such as the continual frieze on the sanctuary, 160 m. long, done in the Ionic manner, the interior colonnade in a "u" shape which housed the gold and ivory statue of the goddess a work by Phidias, the double colonnade on the narrow sides and so on.

Nothing has survived of the religious statue. We know that it was a work by Phidias and that it was made of valuable materials, gold and ivory. It was approximately 12 m. high and it did not rest straight on the floor of the shrine but was set on a rectangular base. The goddess was standing, and wearing a

The east facade of the Parthenon.

helmet, and had a breastplate which was a Medusa's head made of ivory; in her right hand she was holding a Victory while in the other she had a spear.

Leaning against her leg was her great shield and near her spear a snake. Pliny mentions that on the base of the statue was a relief represen- tation of the birth of Pandora where 20 gods were to be found, while on the soles of the god- dess sandals was a depiction of the battle with the Lapiths and the Centaurs.

On the exterior side of the goddess' shield was depicted a battle with the Amazons and on the interior a battle with the Giants. Finally, the body of the goddess was covered with a long, Doric Attican peplos falling in pleats. The form of the statue is know to us today from ancient descriptions, from copies on a smaller scale and from copies of various of its sections in other kinds of works.

The sculptural frieze by itself represents one of Phidias' innovations. He introduced an Ionic element (the frieze) into a Doric temple and thereby started a new tradition. But that is not the only innovation. The subject that is depicted is thought to have been revolutionary because it was far removed from the subjects customarily used for depiction up until then - namely, the ancient, sacred myths - using for its subject contemporary democracy as seen through the course of the Panathenaic Procession. The Panathenaic festival was the greatest of Athenian festivals, held in honor of its protectress goddess, Athena.

A real procession is depicted on the frieze. The astonishing detail, the precision and the plasticity reveal the genius of its creator, Phidias. The theme develops and naturally flows around all four sides of the frieze.

But the visitor can only admire one part of it. Specifically, the monument retains the whole west side (admire the amazing depiction of the startled horse and the horse-trainer) quite a few plaques from the north, and a few from the south.

Two of those from the eastern side of the frieze are in the Acropolis Museum.

But the largest part of the frieze is in the British Museum! The return of these marbles is an ongoing aspiration of the Greeks, initiated by and large, by the efforts of the unforgettable Melina Mercouri.

49

The 92 metopes of the temple are reliefs as well with motifs from the Battle with the Giants, the Battle with the Amazons, the Battles with the Centaurs and scenes from the Trojan War. On the two pediments of the Parthenon, Phidias depicted two myths related to Athena: on the east side her birth from the head of Zeus and on the west her dispute with Poseidon over the occupation of Attica. Most of the sculpture on the east pediment was destroyed before 1674 while on the west side it survived in good condition till it suffered heavy damage from the bombardment of Morosini in 1687.

The sections of the pediment that have survived are today in the Acropolis Museum and the British Museum.

The Temple of Rome and Augustus

This is a small tholos, 8.50 m. in diameter with a perimetric Ionic colonnade of nine columns without a shrine which lies a short way east of the entrance to the Parthenon. On the architrave was an engraved inscription which mentioned that the monument was dedicated by the Athenians to the goddess Rome and the god Augustus. It must have been built a short time after 27 B.C. when Octavius acquired the title of Augustus.

The Sanctuary of Zeus Polieos

NE of the Parthenon are the remains of the temple of Zeus. It consists of a rectangular peribolos and the main temple, which had its own special peribolos and contained a small temple and an altar. A local ceremony was held in the sanctuary in honor of Zeus, Dipolia

The Erechtheion

North of the Parthenon is the second large temple on the Acropolis, the Erechtheion, which is somewhat later. Its construction started in 421 B.C., was halted for the Sicilian Campaign and was completed between 409-405 B.C. Its architect is unknown even though many have maintained it was Mnisiklis. From an inscription of 409/408 B.C. we know the name of an architect who supervised the works at this stage; he was Philoklis and was from the deme of Acharnes. This is a complex and completely original structure. Its name shows it to be the dwelling of Erechtheos and it corresponds to a complex temple building.

The Erechtheion and the Caryatids,
a bold architectural work.

Its architectural peculiarities were the result of the endeavor to leave certain points with religious meaning untouched as well as the endeavor to have a variety of uncommon forms of worship coexisting in the building at one and the same time. It was a pillared building with six columns on the facade, internally divided by a transverse wall into two parts which do not communicate with each other. The two sections of the shrine had a difference of three meters in height and did not communicate with each other. The west side of the building was not enclosed by a wall but had five openings separated by railings with four intermediary Ionic columns which during the Roman period were converted into windows.

The Erechteion of the east pediment
of the Parthenon ("The Birth of Athena").

To the south was the Porch of the Caraytids which was built on the tomb of Kekrops, with six Kores statues which rest on the high continuous base and gracefully support the entablature, of an Asian type, and the marble roof. Five of the statues, which today have been replaced by plaster casts, are found in the Acropolis Museum and one in the British Museum.

On the north side of the west part of the structure a four-pillared entrance porch was fashioned in a "u" shape with six Ionic columns. The entrance door from the north porch into the west apartment of the shrine was particularly well-crafted.

The door, adorned with repeated and profusely decorated motifs, large rosettes and two cornices to the left and the right, is a marvelous example of what the Ionic style was like at the end of the 5th century. Investigators have formulated a number of views regarding the various areas of worship in the Erechtheion.

According to the most prevalent one: the eastern section must have been dedicated to the goddess Athena to which the effigy of the goddess had been transferred part from the older temple while the western must have been used for the worship of Erechtheos as well as Hephaestus and the hero Voutos. The main part of the temple's sculptural decoration has been lost.

The frieze was made of plaques of dark-colored Eleusinian stone on which were secured the relief figures made of pentelic marble. The entire building was constructed of pentelic marble.

The motifs on the frieze have not been clearly deciphered. They most probably reflected the local myths of the town. On the pediments were found the birth of Athena from Zeus' head and the dispute of Poseidon and Athena over the rule of Attica.

Near the Erechtheion is the entrance or the exit of the passage to the Cave of Aglauron Athena where according to mythology the goddess' sacred snake entered and left the Acropolis.

The Pandroseion

This small sanctuary, which was on the west side of the Erechtheion, consisted of a four-sided enclosure containing a small temple, the altar of Erkeios Zeus and the sacred olive tree of Athena. Today only a few ruins remain. The sanctuary was dedicated to Pandrosos, one of the daughters of the mythical founder-king Kekrops. The structure predates the Erechtheion.

The House of the Arrephorai

This is a building that lies near the Erechtheion. It consists of a room and an antechamber with two columns set between pilasters. Pausanias informs us that the Arrephorai lived there, that is, the virgins who took part in secret ceremonies. The Arrephorai must have been connected to a fertility cult.

The Bronze Statue of Athena

There were a host of votive offerings on the sacred rock which were dedicated by towns or ordinary citizens. Of these, the large bronze Athena is of special interest. The statue was erected between the Erechtheion and the Propylaia and with its base was 9 meters high. Pausanias mentions that is was dedicated to Athena Promachus from the tithe of the victory at Marathon against the Persians. The statue made a great impression in antiquity because of its dimensions and as Pausanias informs us the point of the spear and the crest of the helmet of Athena are visible when one approached (Piraeus), sailing from Sounion .

Above: The Caryatids, perhaps the most famous surviving group of sculpture on the Akropolis. They stand guard over the mythical founder of the town, Kerkrops.

Below: General view of Erechtheion.

On the southeast side of the Parthenon is the modern Acropolis Museum. The short space between the temple and the museum is of no particular archaeological interest but it does offer a panoramic view of the south slope of the sacred rock with the Theater of Dionysos spread out at its base.

The museum, whose exhibits are exclusively from the Acropolis, is one of the most important in Greece. There is a small courtyard at its entrance which leads to a wide corridor.

The tour should begin in the room to the left of the corridor so that the chronological develop-ment of the exhibits can be better understood. It contains nine rooms which succeed one ano-ther, and clearly relate the history of Attic art from the Archaic period until the acme of its Classical grandeur in the 5th century B.C.

Masterpieces of Archaic and Classical sculpture are on display, which were architectural deco-rations of the temples on the Acropolis or were offerings made in that space.

There are also porous limestone pediments with depictions of myths from Archaic temples. There is even a Caraytid on display and plaques from the frieze, and metopes and sculptures from the pediments of the Parthenon.

In the Acropolis Museum one can admire the works of the great sculptor of antiquity, Phidias. The renowned Archaic sculptures of women, which were found buried in the Erechtheion and elsewhere, are also exceptional.

In the **first room** one's attention is attracted by two sculptural groups. The first is the oldest pediment from the Acropolis and depicts Heracles with the Lernaian Hydra and the second depicts a lioness who is devouring a bull and a piece of pediment from and Archaic temple (6th century B.C.)

Also of note is a Gorgon's head made of pentelic marble which was the acrotirion of an Archaic temple of Athena (6th century B.C.)

Of particular interest in the **second room** is the Archaic pediment from 580 B.C. with the apotheosis of Heracles to Olympus as well as the pediment of Heracles fighting Triton.

But unquestionably the best exhibit in the room is the "Calf-Bearer", an Archaic statue of a made by Rhombos, according to the inscription of the base.

Above: The triple-Bodied Demon from the pediment of an Archaic temple.

Right page: the "Calf-Bearer" the famous Archaic sculpture in the musuem's second room.

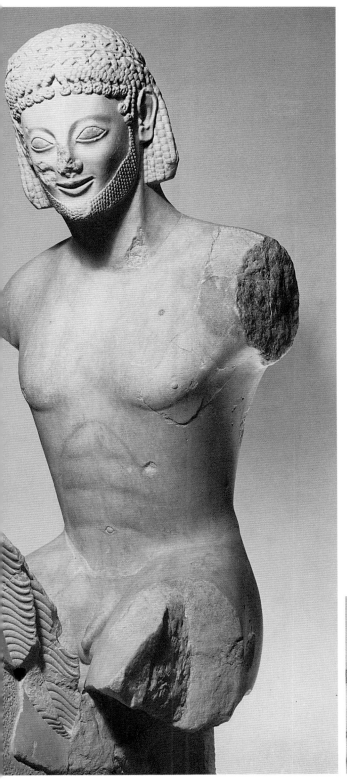

In the **third room** one's attention is claimed by an imposing pediment complex where a bull is being devoured by lions. Also exceptional is a votive sphinx with a sweet expression on its face.

In the first part of the **fourth room** are four works which are attributed to one of the greatest artists of the Archaic period, Phaidimos: the "Horseman" from 560 B.C., the "Peplos Kore" from 530 B.C. which shows particular sensitivity in the execution of the face and the framing of the body with the severe Doric peplos, the statue of a running dog from around 520 B.C. and a spout in the shape of a lion's head which ornamented the temple of Athena during the time of the Peisistratids. In the second part of the room are housed a marvelous collection of Kores which are set up in groups, according to the technique used. They are dated from between 550 and 500 B.C. and are works of sculptors influenced by Ionic art.

Left: The exquisitely expressive Kore no. 674, in the museum's fourth room.

Center: The "Horseman", Archaic sculpture.

Below: Lion's head spout from the Parthenon, 4th room.

In the **fifth room** the visitor will admire pieces from the imposing complexes of the eastern pediment of the old temple of Athena, from the time of the Peisistratids. They depict a Battle with the Giants with the astonishing presence of the goddess Athena in the center of the pediment. The two Victories from the Roman period, made of terracotta, are of especial interest, copies of prototypes from the 5th century B.C.; there is also the Kore by the sculptor Antinoras (end of the 6th century B.C.). In the seven cases in the room are displayed a interesting collection of pottery from various periods.

In the **sixth room** are displayed marvelous works in the so-called "severe style", the technique that was the forerunner of the classical masterpieces.

There are also the relief of the pensive Athena from 460-450 B.C., a head of an ephebe from 485 B.C., a statue of a boy known as the "Kritios Boy", an astonishing marble horse, the "Sulking Kore" from 490 B.C. and a painted panel of terracotta (end of the 6th century B.C.) which was most likely a section of a polyptych or a frieze.

In the **seventh room** is a representation of two pediments of the Parthenon in reduced scale as well as mutilated sections from the frieze of the temple and the west pediment.
The metope where a Centaur is seizing a Lapid is worth note.

In the **eighth room** the visitor will admire several of the masterpieces of the art of all the periods. There are about 20 panels on display from the Ionic frieze of the Parthenon with the procession of the Great Panathenaic Procession as well as relief plaques from the parapet of the temple of Nike where the famed Victory is undoing her sandal.
Works done in the "rich " style with a distinctive casualness and tenderness in the attire which superbly describes the curves of the human body.

In the **ninth room** are displayed four authentic Caraytids from the porch of the Erechtheion These famous sculptures come from the workshop of the sculptor Alkamenis.
On the opposite wall there is interest to be found in a relief depicting a trireme, a mask of Dionysos of colossal size from the Roman period and two marble "kalyptires" from the Parthenon.

Finally, in the **museum's corridor** the statue of Procne and Itys is on display, attributed to Alkamenis, a likeness of Alexander the Great made of pentelic marble, a very expressive head of a philosopher from the first half of the 5th century B.C. and at the exit door a marble owl from the beginning of the 5th century B.C., a symbol of the immortal city of Athens

"The Blond-Haired Boy",
a work from the Classical period, 6th room.

Sections, or slabs, from the frieze of the Parthenon whih show in relif the majestic Panathenaic Procession, the largest and most majestic of all the festival held in Athens of the 5th century B.C. The Panathenaia were established during the rule of Pericles and thus came to symbolize, in the noblest of ways, the city'a great achievements. Economics, science, philoshophy and the arts all reached unheard of levels, creating what today is called the "Golden Age" (Acropolis Museum, room 8).

On the slopes of the sacred rock

Tripodon Street runs along the south slope of the Acropolis. According to Pausanias it started at the Prytaneum of the Ancient Agora and ended after Pericles' Odeon at the Theater of Dionysos.

The Temple and the Theater of Dionysos

Beneath the Acropolis, at the side of Dionysios Aeropagitou Street is the temple of Dionysos Eleftherios and next to it the Theater of Dionysos. **The Temple of Dionysos** was built in the 5th century B.C. Its rectangular foundation still survives and on it was placed the gold and ivory statue of the god, a work by Alkamenis, a student of Phidias.

It was found within a shrine enclosed by a peribolos. Near this larger temple are the remains of the foundations of the oldest temple which must have been double-columned, that is, enclosed between two door-posts. In the 4th century B.C. a Doric stoa was built to the north of the shrine against the back of which the structure of the theater stage rested.

The Theater of Dionysos, detail from the bema of Phaedros.

The **Theater of Dionysos** comes after the temple; its orchestra forms a perfect circle. This orchestra is of particular significance for the history of civilization. It was the main orchestra of Athens, the cradle of the dramatic art of both the ancient and the more recent world.

Here the tragedies of Aeschylus, Sophocles and Euripides, as well as the comedies of Aristophanes and Menandros, were preserved for the first time. The Theater of Dionysos took on its definitive form at the end of the 4th century B.C. when it was renovated by Lykourgos an art lover, orator and archon of Athens. To the north of the theater, near the wall of the Sacred Rock, are the remains of the choragic monument o Thrasyllos, who was the "benefactor" of the Dionysian performances. Later, after the victory of his son Thrasyklis in 297 B.C., the monument was modified. Today, in the cavity that is formed in the rock there is the chapel to the **Panayia Spiliotissa** ("Virgin Mary of the Cave").

Right page, above:
View of the Theater of Dionysos.
Below: The bema of Phaedros as seen
from the theater's stage.

The Asclepeion

On the northwest side of the Theater of Dionysos is the sanctuary of Asclepeios (the Asclepeion). It contains the three buildings necessary for the worship of the god: the temple, the stoa where worshippers slept awaiting miraculous dreams and a sacred spring. The god/doctor Asclepeios treated the sick by the method of incubation.

In the temple were the statues of Asclepeios and his daughter Hygeia. In the middle of the north wall of the stoa, which served as the incubation site, there was an opening which led to a cave in the rock. Here was the spring of purified water , an element essential to the operation of the sanctuary. The cave that lies above the Asclepeion was transformed into a church during the Byzantine period, the Panayia Chrysokastriotissa (the Virgin Mary Chrysokastriotissa). Further west are the foundations of two small buildings, a temple dedicated to Themis and a sanctuary dedicated to Aphrodite.

The Stoa of Eumenis

West of the Theater of Dionysos and extending up to the Odeon of Herod Atticus was a large stoa with a Doric colonnade on its facade and an interior Ionic colonnade. The stoa was created as a gift of the king of Pergamon Eumenis II (196-159 B.C.) who was a student in Athens during his childhood and who admired the intellectual glory of the town. It was used for the protection of the citizens from adverse weather conditions as well as a gathering place. Next to it are the remains of the choragic monument of Nikias of Nikodimos which was dedicated to his victory in the choragia of 319 B.C.

The Odeon of Pericles

East of the Theater of Dionysos lies the famous Pericles Odeon built in 447 B.C. and used for musical competitions. From the excavations it appears to have been a large hypostyle room with wooden idols in the interior and it was destroyed by fire in 86 B.C.

The Odeon of Herod Atticus

The Odeon of Herod Atticus was built in 16 B.C. by the eminent Athenian orator and philosopher Herod Atticus, in memory of his wife Rigillis. The Odeon is in the shape of a theater because it was used for theatrical, as well as musical, presentations.

The Herodeon has a circular orchestra and a forestage which is 35.40 m. long, 1.10 m. high and 6 m. deep. There are recesses in the stage wall where there were statues. The orchestra is laid with polychrome tiles. The Odeon holds 5,000 spectators. Above the cornice there was a stoa, the theater's present foyer. The Odeon was roofed with a luxurious cedar. It must have been one of the most brilliant structures of the period of Pausanias. It stayed in use until perhaps the invasion of the Heruli (267 B.C.). The Herodeon experienced many vicissitudes and disasters. It the end it burned down. This can be seen from the burned pieces of wood and the nails that were found during excavations in the last century. Today it is one of the most important open spaces for cultural events. During the summer it is used for concerts in the context of the Athens Festival. Superb presentations of ancient and modern drama are also staged in the Herod Atticus Theater. A brilliant adornment for Athens, it also constitutes an important award for the artist Greek or foreign, who presents his work there. Every year it is inundated with spectators and most of its events are considered cultural landmarks.

The Herod Atticus Theater.
Today it plays host to many very
important cultural events.

5

ANCIENT MONUMENTS

Around the Acropolis

The history of Attica and its basin is the source of the unique monuments on the sacred rock of At-hens, which is crow-ned by the temple of Athena, the Parthenon. But the love of the Athenians for the arts, for beauty in all things and above all for their city, expressed itself in dozens of other monuments that radiate from the Acropolis. These are historical sites such as the **Ancient Agora** where the concept of democracy was born and came to maturity as a form of government and which contains many other noteworthy sites such as the **Stoa of Attalos.** The **Museum of the Agora** has on display the objects found there as well as many other important exhibits. The **Roman Agora** with **Hadrian's Library** and the **Tower of the Winds** ornament the nighborhood of Plaka while the **Theseio**, the temple of Hephaestus, which gave its name to another picturesque quarter, complements the view of the Acropolis. Next to it is **Kerameikos**, the town's ancient cemetery, which by itself could tell us of all the triumphal

and difficult moments Athens has experienced. In the **Kerameikos Museum** are displayed several of the most important funerary steles from the area. A bit further on is the **Hill of Philopappou** with its museum dedicated to the Muses with a superb view of both the Acropolis and the Saronic Gulf, a view that can also be enjoyed from the Hill of the Nymphs and the **Planetarium**. To the east of the rock of the Acropolis is the **Temple of Olympian Zeus,** and **Hadrian's Arch** as well as the ancient **Stadium** which was renovated in the 19th century to play host to the first modern Olympic Games in 1896. Finally, on the north side of the Acropolis are the **Areos pagos** and the **Pnyx,** where the first democratic assemblies in the history of mankind were held. Strolling among these monuments, which are a natural continuation of the Acropolis, is an extremely impressive experience and will attract the visitor who is searching for the echoes of the ancient city that have still survived down to the present.

The Ancient Agora

The Agora was the most important part of every city-state in ancient Greece. It was the center of life, of economic, social, political and judicial activity, as well as the main commercial center ("agora" is from ageiro = to assemble).

The Ancient Agora of Athens covers an area of only 40 stremmata (approximately 10 acres). It lies below the Acropolis south of the hill of the Areios Pagos and west of the hill of Agoraios Kolonos. Excavations have shown that this area has been continuously inhabited since the Neolithic period (3,000 B.C.).

After the destruction of the site by the Persians the sanctuaries and the various other buildings were rebuilt. The western part of the agora was the intellectual center of the city. In 15 B.C. the Odeon or concert hall was here as well as the temple of Ares. During the first two centuries after Christ other buildings were added and the Agora reached its zenith.

The north side of the Ancient Agora

On the north side of the Ancient Agora are the ruins of a structure known as the Basilica, from the 2nd century A.D., and a portico from a civic building from the 1st century A.D. Here are also the remains of the Poikili Stoa. It was erected in the 5th century B.C. with a Doric colonnade on the facade and an Ionic one in the interior. It was a highly frequented stoa and owed its name to the paintings that decorated it. In this building the Thirty Tyrants imposed the death penalty on about 1,500 citizens. The philosopher Zeno, whose adherents were called Stoics, also taught there.

The Central area of the Ancient Agora

In the central area of the Ancient Agora are the ruins of the **Leokoreon**. A sanctuary in honor of the daughters of the Attica hero Leo who gave their life to save Athens from the plague. South of the Poikili Stoa are the ruins of the **Altar of the Twelve Gods** and even further south the **Temple** and the **Altar of Aris**. In the center of the market was the **Odeon of Agrippa**, which was started in 15 B.C. and originally was used for musical events; later it was used as a place for lectures. It was destroyed in 267 A.D. and the **Gymnasium** was built on its ruins; it was not only used for athletics but for education and entertainment as well. The entire central space of the agora was full of votive offerings.

The West Side of the Ancient Agora

The **Basileios Stoa**, was where the prince-king had his seat. It was constructed in the 6th century B.C. and had a Doric colonnade on its facade and a second one in the interior. Perhaps this is where Solon's laws were set, inscribed on triangular tablets.

The Stoa of Zeus Eleftherios was built in the 5th century B.C. and had a Doric colonnade on its facade and a second Ionic one in the interior. The stoa served the public and social life of the Athenians.

The paintings and the mosaics found there show that it functioned as a gathering place for political and philosophical discussions.

The Temple of Apollo Patroos lies next to the preceding stoa and was built in the 4th century B.C. The statue of the god was erected in the temple shrine.

There was a small temple just to the north of this dedicated to the worship of **Zeus Phatrios** and **Athena Phatria**.

South of the temple of Apollo is the **Metroon** from the 2nd century B.C. In its rooms, the original votes cast in the Boule were stored in cupboards. The middle room of the Mitroos was the temple of Rhea, the Mother of the Gods.

Next to it was the old **Bouleuterion.**

The New Bouleuterion was the building where the sessions of the Athenian Parliament of the 500 were held after the Peloponnesian wars. At a distance of approximately 10 meters south of the Metroon are the remains of the Tholos know as Skia (in this case, parasol) It was erected between 470-460 B.C.

The Tholos was the seat of the Prytanes and housed the keys to the temples, the originals of the weights and measures, the shrine of the city-state and the state seal.

The facade of the Stoa of Attalos, where the Museum of the Ancient Agora is housed.

Monuments on the east side

On the east side of the Ancient Agora are the ruins of the **Northeast Stoa** and a **Library** which was built in 100 A.D. The east side of the Ancient Agora was enclosed by a large stoa, the Stoa of King Attalos II.

The Stoa of Attalos

It was built by the King of Pergamon Attalos II (159-138 B.C.) and served both for commercial exchanges and a place for Athenians to divert themselves. The stoa had a double colonnade and in the back part shops on the first floor with the same arrangement on the ground floor. On the facade there were 45 Doric columns and in the interior 22 Ionic columns. It constitutes a typical example of a stoa structure from the Hellenistic period.

The Museum of the Ancient Agora

The **Museum** of the Ancient Agora is housed in the reconstructed Stoa of Attalos. It contains the finds from the excavations in the Agora.
There are also works on display from the Neolithic, Protohelladic, Mesohelladic and Mycenean periods.

There is also sculpture from the Archaic, Classical, Hellenistic and Roman periods, Archaic ceramics, black-figured and red-figured vases, and copper and clay idols from all periods. Furthermore, there are collections of amphoras, utensils of everyday use, and oil lamps from all the above periods, as well as objects from public life and important inscriptions. There are mosaics from the 4th century B.C. and Byzantine pottery.

The south side of the Ancient Agora

On the south side of the Agora are found:
The Middle Stoa: It was built in the 2nd century B.C. and had an orignal form.
The view has been put forward that it served the needs of the courts, most probably the large popular court of Helliaia. It was started and paid for by Attalos I and was completed by his sons. Near it are the ruins of the **Southwest Fountain** and the **Triangular Sanctuary.** Other noteworthy buildings in the area are the **Enneakrouno** (The Nine Fountains), a work by the Peisistratids, the **Mint of Athens** and the **Nymphaeon**.

The Theseio, or the Temple of Hephaestus

At the peak of Agoraios Kolonos hill is the best preserved temple of antiquity, the Theseio.

The Theseio or the temple of Hephaestus, is a peripteral temple, the same as the Parthenon. It was built with pentelic marble. It has 13 columns on its long side and 6 on its narrow. The feats of Heracles and Theseus are engraved in relief on its metopes.

The Theseio was built during the time of Pericles. After 1821, it was the only closed and covered space usable as a museum: the first national archaeological museum of modern Greece. During the early years of Christianity the Theseio was converted into the church of Saint George.

There was also a square building on the same hill known as the **Skevothiki,** a small sanctuary from the 2nd century B.C, that was dedicated to Demos and the Three Graces.

The temple of Hephaestos in the Ancient Agora.

The Roman Agora

Lying east of the Ancient Agora, the Roman Agora was created in the 1st century A.D. to serve a growing Athens. It constitutes a self-sufficient space and is entered from Aiolou Street.

Among its well-known buildings is the Agoranomeion for the Market Authorities, the Portico, and the Gate of Athena Archigetis. This gate was built by Julius Caesar in honor of Athena.

The Tower of the Winds (The Temple of Aiolos)

The **Tower of the Winds** is found in the Roman Agora. This is an octagonal tower which was built by the astronomer Andronikos from Kyrrhos in Syria. It was created as a meteorological station and clock. Thus, today this building is also called The Clock of Andronikos, or even the Temple of Aiolos. The clock, made of marble, was built in the shape of a octagonal tower and the roof was pyramidal.

Right page: The Roman Agora and the Tower of the Winds. Above: representations of the winds from the reliefs on the Tower of the Winds.

At the top of the pyramid was placed a revolving copper Triton which showed the direction of the wind. On the frieze of the monument were carved depictions of the eight winds: Boreas (north), Sciron (southwest), Zephyr (west), Apeliotis (east), Livas (south), Notos (south) Evros (southeast) and Kaikias (northeast).

High up, in the corners on the sides, were iron rods with carved lines that indicated the hours of the day, when there was sunlight. Inside the tower was a water-clock which showed the time when there was not any sun, an invention of Andronikos. South of the tower are the ruins of the **Agoranomeio** from the 1st century A.D. It has a monumental facade and a wide staircase leading up to it.

Above: The entrance to the Roman Agora.

Below: The Ancient and the Roman Agora.

Hadrian's Library

Hadrian's Library was one of the largest buildings in Athens. It is often characterized as a gigantic rectangle (122 x 82 m.) with high, strong walls. During ancient times Hadrian's Library was here and according to Pausanias had 100 columns of Phrygian stone, residences with gilding and alabaster roofs, decorated with statues and paintings. Inside was where the books were kept.

The Hill of the Nymphs (the Planetarium)

On the southwest side of ancient Athens is the Hill of the Nymphs at a height of 147 m. Because the area was dedicated to the Nymphs, we are led to the conclusion that it must have once been verdant and idyllic. Today the building housing the National Planetarium is there, a neoclassical structure from the 19th century.

Areopagos (the rock of Ares)

To the northwest of the Acropolis rises up the rock of the Areopagos and its grove. Here is where the Council of Nobles or the High Council of the Areos Pagos, the old political body of the Athenians, convened. Here is also where the Apostle Paul came to proclaim the new religion in 54 A.D. - Christianity. A plaque with his proclamation has been placed on the base of the rock.

The Pnyx

Opposite the small grove of the Areopagos, and alongside Apostolos Pavlos Street between the hills of the Muses and the Nymphs, is the Pnyx hill, with an enormous man-made semicircular flat space with a bema, a speaker's platform for orators, on top. For the ancient Athenians the Pnyx was what the parliament of a democratic country is today. Athens called its Parliament the "Assembly of the Deme". Here the great orators such as Demosthenes or Aeschines delivered their speeches. The institutions needed for their democratic governing of a people were born and developed on the Pnyx. Today international events which have to do with democracy, in all its aspects, are held on the hill of the Pnyx.

Section of the Monument to the Muses on the hill of Philopappou.

The Hill of the Muses (Philopappou)

Opposite the Acropolis and west of the gate, is the small hill of Philopappou, a verdant place with pathways, perfect for a stroll. The hill took its name from the funeral monument that was erected there on its peak in 119 A.D., in memory of the Philhellene Gaius Julius Antiochos Philopappos. Philopappos was a Roman monarch from Syria. He was a great benefactor of the town of Athens during that time. This was a sacred hill in ancient Athens. The monument was dedicated to the Muses and called the Mouseion. It was a square building 10 m. wide. The side facing the Acropolis formed a semicircular arch, turned outward. This is the only part that has survived. In the recess of the monument, which is 10 m. high, were the statues of the family of Philopappos and himself. The view from up here is spectacular, both toward the Acropolis and toward the Saronic Gulf. Going up Dionysios Aeropagitou Street you encounter right at the start of the flagstoned street leading into Philopappou, the small chapel of Ayios Dimitrios Loumbardiaris.

Kerameikos

The entrance to the Kerameikos archaeological site is on Ermou Street just beyond Asomaton Square, next to the electric train station of Theseio.

When in 478 B.C. the first walls of Athens were being built this place was a section of the ancient deme of Keramaies and was divided into two parts: the inner Kerameikos inside the town and the outer Kerameikos to the west, outside the town walls.

The name Kerameikos comes from the "Kerameis", those who were involved with the moulding of clay, potters. Inner Kerameikos had good quality clay; and the artists used it to make the renowned ceramics of Attica.

These two areas, Inner and Outer Kerameikos, were connected by two gates in the wall, the Sacred Gate and the Dipylos Gate. The road to Eleusis began at the Sacred Gate. This road was named the Sacred Way because it was used for the procession of the Eleusinian Mysteries. The road to Piraeus began at the Dipylos Gate, and the Panathenaic Procession set off from here and went all the way to the Propylaia. The Outer Kerameikos was the cemetery of Athens from prehistoric to historic times. The road toward Plato's Academy, which was located further down, was lined on both sides with monuments of the most eminent men of the city. Here were found the tombs of Thrasyboulos, Pericles, Chavrios, Phormion, Kleisthenis and others.

The Eridanos river flowed alongside the Gate of the Sacred Way, having its source on Hymettus near Kaisariani. Sections of the walls of the Themistoclean enclosure have survived at Kerameikos. The Street of the Tombs is 8 m. wide and 90 m. long.

The most important monuments there are the Nikistratis and the Kifisdoros memorials, the Lysimachides monument showing a boat being rowed by Charon, and the Dionysios monument in the shape of a proud bull.

Funerary monuments and a view of Keramikos, the cemetary of ancient Athens.

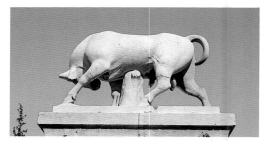

The Kerameikos Museum

The museum found at Kerameikos has on display finds from the excavations of the German Archaeological Institute.
Here one can admire the most important funerary monuments from Archaic and Classical times. There are lavish collections of ceramics from the sub-Mycenean to the Roman period, idols, bronze and glass objects and other tomb offerings. There is an important collection of pots, statues, bases, columns, shards and gold wreathes.

The Olympieion

The Columns of the Temple of Olympian Zeus rise up in one of the most beautiful settings in Athens. This area, because of its proximity to the Ilissos river, has been inhabited since prehistoric times. Here was the center of the town, and where tradition places the residence of King Aegeus and the oldest sanctuaries such as the sanctuary of Olympian Zeus, the Pythion, the sanctuary of Ge (Gaia) and the Dionysios en Limnais (Dionysios on the Lake). According to Pausanias, Athenian tradition said the site was connected to the myth of the creation of the human race. The founder of the sanctuary of Zeus is thought to have been Deukalion, he and Pyrrha were the only human beings to survive the great flood.

The temple that was built here was one of the largest in Greece and the largest in the Corinthian style. Its foundations were laid by Peisistratos in the 6th century B.C. It was completed in the 2nd century A.D. by Hadrian. The temple is built on a large rectangle, 250 m. long and 130 m. wide.

On the north side there was a Portico with four columns and the main entrance. The temple is dipteral with eight columns. Today 16 columns have survived of the original total of 108. Of these, one has been lying on the ground since being hit by a bolt of lighting in 1852. The columns are 17.25 m. high and have a diameter at their base of 1.70 m. with 20 flutings. Inside the temple there was a gold and ivory statue of Zeus. It was one of the Seven Wonders of the ancient world. The Roman sage Livy said that the temple of Zeus in Athens is the only one in the world conceived on a scale equal to the majesty of the great god. In the temple's enormous enclosure there was a veritable forest of statues.

Hadrian's Gate

Hadrian's Gate lies at the intersections of Syngrou, Dionysios Areopagitou and Amalias Avenues. This gate was built by Hadrian in 131 A.D. and functioned as a triumphal arch. It is a large arched gate 18 m. high, 13 m. wide and 2.30 m. deep.

Oposite page: Views from the ruins of the Olympeion, the grand temple dedicated to Zeus.

The Stadium

The ancients built their stadiums on the slopes of hills near the towns. Thus the Panathinakos Stadium was built on Ardittus hill next to the Ilissos river. In 330 B.C. Lykourgos built this stadium of stone. In 140 A.D. Herod Atticus renovated it, adding marble and a majestic propylaia. The track has a length of 204 m. and a width of 33.36 m. The course was marked out in herms instead of ordinary distance markers, in other words with square columns with the busts of Dionysios and Apollo. Only four of these columns have been found. The Panathenaic Games were held in the stadium and included all the usual contests. The winner's trophy was an amphora which contained olive oil from Athena's olive tree. The Romans converted the stadium into a gladiator's arena. Later the stadium was deserted. In modern Greece, the entire stadium was redressed with marble at the expense of the philanthropist Giorgos Averof. In 1896, with the revival of the institution of the Olympics, the first modern games were held here at the initiative of Baron Pierre Coubertin, 1,500 years after the final ancient games were held. Today it continues to be one of the most important athletic installations in the country. Major athletic events are held there and recently important cultural events as well.

The Panathenaikos Stadium, today.

6

OLD ATHENS

Plaka - Monastiraki

The term "old" used for a city like Athens can, of course, only be a relative one. It refers to the way the city looked in the 19th century with its ancient, Byzantine, Ottoman and neo-classical elements in the neighborhoods around the Acropolis and Lycabettus and, more generally, wherever the city was built up. Liberation from the Turks and the creation of an independent Greek state was the definitive factor in this image, the image that the visitor still enjoys today. The building of the Palace (the present Parliament building), the Old Parliament, the University and the National Library, the Zappeion and the National Technical School, as well as the Panathinaikos Stadium and the National Museum, created an axis of life between two large settlements: Theseio and Plaka on the one hand and Exarcheia, Neapoli and Kolonaki on the other. Furthermore, the industries that sprang up to the south, gave a new air to the then western suburbs such as Omonoia, Metaxourgeio and

Kolonos. Today the exhibition site at Gazi is a dominant feature of the area. If we take into account the rapid development of the new capital economically, which can be seen from the spread of Kolonaki, Pangrati and the area around the First Cemetery (Kynosargos) it becomes obvious how complex Athens was in the 19th century, socially, economically and - above all else - culturally. However, Athens still retained, by remaining faithful to the historical traces of its past, the same beauty and the same value for its inhabitants. And that is why even today when it has spilled outside the Attica basin it still attracts the visitor to this town of spirit, even in its simple, perhaps under-developed neighborhoods. Whether one happens to be in Metaxourgeia, Kolonos or Petralona, or stays in Plaka with its houses and shops, so colorful and bustling, or moves through the beautiful lanes of Monastiraki, he is invited to discover the same beauties, whether they prove easy or hard to find.

Plaka

The neighborhood of the Gods as Greeks and foreigners alike have dubbed it, singing its praises. Plaka is for Athens what Covent Gardens is for London or Montmartre for Paris. Located on the northeastern slopes of the rock of the Acropolis, Plaka was the center of Athens even in antiquity. The famed Panathenaic procession passed along Tripodon St., still a part of present day Plaka. The area took its present form after the proclamation of Athens as the newly constituted Greek state, when the excavations also began.

Then builders came in from the Cyclades, from the island of Anafi in particular, in order to work on the excavations. In order to have a place to sleep at night they built their humble dwellings under the rock of the Acropolis, and thus that neighborhood took the name "Ta Anafiotika". The architecture and the lanes in Anafiotika are reminiscent of the Cyclades. The area slowly filled with narrow streets, many of which take you back to where you started off with detached houses built in a neoclassical style, houses at the most two-storey with tiny courtyards that smell of vervain and basil.

You enter the interior of Plaka from Mitropoleos and Nikis St. where the Ministry of Education is today. Going along Nikis St. you will cross Navarchou Nikodimou St and then Thoukididou. There is a small church there, Ayia Rinoula, an old Byzantine building. On the corner of Navarchou Nikodimou and Adrianou Sts., there is a neoclassical style building. This is a school that was built in 1875.

Above: The church of "St. George of the Rock" in Anafiotika, below the Acropolis.

Below: A lane in Anafiotika, typical of a Cycladic street lay-out.

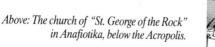

Adrianou St. is the largest and most central in Plaka and has had a commercial character since the time of King Othon. At No. 98 you turn toward the Gymnasium of Diogenis which was built in the 3rd century B.C. At the corner of Erechtheos and Erotokritou Sts. is the small Byzantine church of St. John the Theologian, a building from the 9th century A.D., in a tiny area with trees, small cafes and tavernas. On the right side of Erechtheos St. is the entrance to the Monastery of Panayia Tafou (the Virgin Mary of the Tomb) and the church of Ayioi Anargyroi (Sts. Kosmas and Damon, 17th century). From Erechtheos St. you turn left toward Prytaneiou St. There is found the Ayios Nikolaos Rangavas (St. Nikolaos Rangavas) church from the 11th century. On the east side of the Rangavas church, walking on Epicharmou St., you enter Anafiotika. There you find Ayios Georgios tou Vrachou (St. George of the Rock) and Ayios Symeon (St. Simeon). To your right is Mnisikleos St. which ends at the Acropolis. It is one of the narrowest streets in Plaka and is stepped at many places, and full of small tavernas with melodic music. From Mnisikleos you turn onto Lysiou St. and from there go to Markou Auriliou St. There you will find the church of Ayios Spyridonas, a building from the 17th century. On the same street is the Panayia Chrysokastriotissa (Our Lady of the Golden Castle), a large church with a courtyard. The street exits on Tholou St where there are a lot of bars. Here is also found the first modern Greek University. It was inaugurated by King Othon in May 1837. It had four schools in the beginning: Theological, Legal, Philosophical and Medical. In 1841 it began to empty because the new university was being slowly completed. Later the ground floor was turned into a taverna, called The "Old University". The building was appropriated and starting in the Seventies works began on its renovation.

Today it is an adornment of Athens and is used as a Museum of Education. On the upper side of the museum is Theorias St. with the small church of the Metamorfosis tou Sotiros (Transfiguration of the Savior), a building from the Venetian period of Athens.

Adrianou St.
typical of the picturesque winding lanes of Plaka.

You are now on the "Peripatos" (Promenade) the road that goes around the Acropolis.
You head down, following the ancient ruins of the Panathenaic Procession, the large Roman wall and the Eleusinian wall. Opposite them is the small church of Ayia Anna (St. Ann) with a beautiful little garden situated on an uphill slope. Then you reach the large church of the Taxiarchs with the Roman Agora next to it, the Tower of the Winds and the start of Aiolou St. This is where the Mendreses is, on Pelopidou St., a Turkish seminary from the 18th century. The Museum of Folk Instruments in on this street. One step further and just off Aiolou you reach a large square with tavernas, cafeterias and abundant greenery. Opposite is the large Hadrian's library, a section of which has been reconstructed, built of pentelic marble, and further down is Monastiraki Square, with the church of the Panayia Pantanassa (the Virgin Mary of All Things).

Above: Itinerant musicians add yet another pleasnt aspect to th Plaka scene.

Below: The Lysikratos Monument.

The Folk Art Museum is located on Kydathinaion St. It contains exceptional collections of objects from the traditional art of the 18th and 19th century as well as the Byzantine period.

Opposite lies the church of the Sotiros (the Savior) from the 12th century. Kydathinaion St. also has the bustling Philomouseiou Etaireia Square, surrounded by outdoor cafeterias, tavernas and ouzo bars. The Philomousos Etaireia, an intellectual center from the 19th century, has had its seat there since 1813.

Finally, from Farmaki St., you can reach Lysikratous St. with the church of Ayia Katerina (St. Catherine).

This is a lovely little chapel from the 12th century whose original form has been altered by numerous additions and repairs. At the intersection of Lysikratous and Shelley Sts. is the choragic monument of Lysikratis. This is a square pedestal which supports a small tholos and was built in 334 B.C. Ancient Tripodon St. passed by here. **Plaka is unique, and extremely colorful, full of tavernas, wine shops, cafeterias, squares, trees, columns, churches, tourists, barrel organs and bars.** Plaka can hold you captive for many hours and even days. Countless shops line your way and offer souvenirs.

This is also a center for artists.

A visitor is bound to find something to buy. Bound to sit somewhere and relax, to drink a cup of Greek coffee or eat Greek delicacies in one of the many little tavernas Plaka has to offer. Plaka is also where Carnival is celebrated in Athens and spring is a festive occasion with flower bedecked balconies and verandas.

Pandrosou St. is the most colorful street in Athens. Thousands of foreigners and Athenians pass through it daily or take a stroll along this street that connects Metropolis Square with Monastiraki Square. It is lined along both sides with shops. Most of these are flush with the northern wall of Hadrian's Library.

Monastiraki

Monastiraki Square lies at the end of Pandrosou St. According to one account it owes its name to the church of the Panayia (the Virgin Mary) there which is a monastic estate of the Kaisariani Monastery whose medieval name was the Great Monastery. Next to it is the electric train station that joins Piraeus to Kifissia. Monastiraki begins at Monastiraki Square, goes down to Ayios Philippas square, and along Ermou St. to Theseio, and Piraeos St. and peters out in the surrounding narrow side streets. At its center lies Avyssinias (Abyssinia) Square which with its junk shops has been the place where the Sunday bazaar has been held since 1910. Yiousouroum, as the area of Monastiraki is called, had always been the bazaar, decked out in its gaudy colors. Everyone here talks to you about art. Whatever they have to sell is a work of art. Of course, there are shops with real antiques. Leaving that aside, it is relaxing to walk through Monastiraki even if you do not buy anything.

Today Monastiraki is a true fair for the one who strolls through it. Thousands and thousands of things are for sale. You can find everything there. Opposite the train lines and the Ancient Agora are Adrianou St. and the square around the church of Ayios Philippas (St. Philip, 17th century) which is full of ouzo bars and traditional cafes. Further down, is Astingos St. with many blacksmiths.

Hephaestou St. buzzes with life and all kinds of shops selling ceramics and weavings, and with junk shops as well.

Commercial activity continues on Ermou St. The middle of it is dominated by the Kapnikarea church and the chapel of Ayia Varvara (St. Barbara). Today the church belongs to the University of Athens. On the right side of Ermou St. is the Cathedral of Athens and next to it the church of Ayios Eleftherios (p. 99).

Monastiraki, below the Acropolis, with fascinating people and shops, remnants of the bygone days.

7

The heart of the modern capital houses the most important buildings connected to Greek culture and intellectual achievement. **Syntagma Square**, the center of Athens, lies in front of the **Greek Parliament Building** and the **Tomb of the Unknown Soldier** which attracts countless tourists every day. Next to them are the **National Gardens**, which stretch all the way to the **President's Mansion**, the **Panathenaic Stadium** and the **Zappeion**, providing a breath of fresh air in an area so much in need of it. There is heavy commercial activity from **Kolonaki** to **Omonoia** and along **Patission St.** where there is another large park, **The Pedion tou Areos**, filled with Athenians, both young and old.

The sky of Attica rests of the hills of **Lycabettus** and **Strefis**, also verdant areas, while at their base the night life of the **Exarcheia** area is in tune with the rhythm of the rest of the town, that is, it goes on till dawn because the areas described in this section never sleep.

Syntagma Square

Syntagma Square is the center of Athens. Here is found the Greek Parliament building and all Greek distances are measured from here in kilometers. The square has many embassies and ministries, the offices of airlines and large companies, banks and luxury hotels. Near the square are the National Gardens and behind them the President's Mansion. Syntagma Square is the center of tourism in Athens. Visitor interest is centered on the monument to the **"Unknown Soldier"** where the changing of the guard, made up of Evzones, who guard it day and night, is an impressive sight especially when seen with the flocks of pigeons flying up and around them.

The Parliament on Syntagma Square with Mt. Lycabettus in the background.

The Parliament

The present-day **Greek Parliament** building lies above the Monument to the Unknown Soldier. It was the Palace of King Othon and Queen Amalia and was built between 1834-1838. The plans were drawn up by the German architect Getner. This three-storey building is constructed of pentelic marble and limestone. It has Doric style propylaia, both small and large rooms, the Parliament assembly hall, the Parliament library and the offices of the State Council.

The Parliament building is surrounded by the National Gardens which has entrances on all four sides and stretches from the Stadium to the Zappeion.

The National Gardens

The **National Gardens** were formerly for the exclusive use of the Palace. Now they are open to everyone. Antiquities have been found there which have been fenced in. There are flower beds, little paths, lofty trees, ponds, playgrounds, little bridges, stone and metal kiosks, statues and many benches to rest on. On the eastern side of the National Gardens, along Herodou Attikou St., is the New Palace, now the Presidential Mansion, the residence of the President of the Republic of Greece. The President's Mansion was designed by the great architect Ernest Ziller.

The Zappeion

The **Zappeion** Megaron is today one of the most up-to-date centers for Greek and international conferences. The Doric columns of its facade, its imposing atrium, and the steps up to the main entrance stand out against the dark green of the pathways making the majesty of the building even more apparent. Athenians love to stroll in the area around the Zappeion.

Its little paths are where groups of Athenians hold sessions of their outdoor Parliaments, attempting to solve the country's problems, on the model of the outdoor Parliament of Hyde Park in London.

Lycabettus

Lycabettus is always beautiful.
You can climb it throughout the year
and enjoy the superb view that it offers
of all points of the city. Either on foot up
the flight of stairs, or by car to the theater
or on the funicular railway from Kolonaki,
all the way to the top (275 m.).
During antiquity it was called Aychesmos
Lycabettus. During the time of Pausanias
Aychesmos Lycabettus had a statue of Zeus
Aychesmios at its summit. Lycabettus hill
is mentioned in Aristophanes' "Clouds"
and in Plato's "Critias".
During the Middle Ages there was a chapel
to Profitis Ilias (The Prophet Elijah) at its summit.
Today there is a chapel to Ayios Georgios
(St. George) which was built after 1835 when
Athens had become the capital of Greece.
On its NW side is a cave with the small church
of Ayios Isidoros (St. Isidore).
During the summer the Lycabettus Theater
plays host to various theatrical performances
and concerts. It is a spacious theater with 5,000
seats and occupies one of the most
aweinspiring and idyllic sites in Athens.

Kolonaki

The chic square of Athens is Kolonaki
officially known as Philikis Etaireias Square.
The square and the surrounding streets have
the most expensive stores in Athens and many
pastry-shops, cafeterias and bistros.
The Gennadios Library is on Soudias St,
and specializes in Greek publications after
1453. **The Museum of Cycladic Art** is housed
on Neophytou Douka St.
The funicular railway that goes to the top
of Lycabettus is in the Kolonaki area.

Right, above: The Parliament Building (Old Palace).
Center: View of the National Gardens.
Below: The Zappeion, next to the National Gardens.

Right above: Mt. Lycabettus.
Below: Kolonaki, the oldest and most aristocratic section
of the modern city of Athens.

Panepistimiou St.

If you take Panepistimiou Avenue (or Eleftherios Venizelos as it is officially named) from Syntagma Square toward Omonoia you will see many historical buildings, all in a row. On the left is the **Grande Bretagne** hotel built to the plans of Hansen. A bit further down and opposite is the Iliou Melathron which has been renovated and houses the Numismatic museum. It was built by Ernest Ziller for the excavator of Mycenae and Troy, **Heinrich Schliemann**. On the same side of the street and further down is the Catholic Church of Ayios Dionysios (St. Denis). This is followed by the Opthalmialogical Hospital built in a Byzantine style and opposite that the Bank of Greece. The next building is the neoclassical building of the Agricultural Bank and opposite that the Athens Academy.

The **Academy** is a work by the Greek Baron Sinas built on the plans of Hansen and under the supervision of Ziller, and done in an Ionic Style. There is the main building and two wings, and pediments depicting the birth of Athena. Apollo and Athena are on the two large Ionic columns. The statues of Socrates and Plato are in front.

The **National University**, founded in 1837, is the middle building on the street. It has propylaia with wall paintings of the renaissance of the arts and sciences in Greece. The Festival Hall is majestic. Statues have been erected in front of the university.

The **National Library**, the third great megaron here is a building in the Doric style and contains over one million volumes of books, manuscripts, gospels and archetypals. Diagonally opposite the library is the renovated Arsakeio where the Council of State is housed. Going down Panepistimiou St. you reach the large Square of Omonoia.

Above: The statues of Apollo and Athena outside the Academy.
Center: The first building from the University of Athens, built in 1837.
Below: Partial view of the Athens Academy.

Right page, above: The Athens Academy.
Below: Panoramic view of the National Library.

Academias Street

Academias St. is the next one up from Panepistimiou St. and runs parallel to it. The Cultural Center of the Municipality of Athens is here. This building, a true gem from the 19th century, is host to many cultural events. The **Theatrical Museum of Athens** and the **Public Library** are housed in the Cultural Center. In the park in front of the center are the statues of the great Greek poet Kostis Palamas and a Sibyl. Academias St. starts at Vasilisas Sofias Boulevard near Syntagma and ends at bustling Kaningos Square.

Stadiou Street - The Museum of Athens

Below the university is Stadiou St which begins at Syntagma Square.

It is one of the three large streets that were laid out in the town-plan of 1832 by the young architects Stamatis Kleanthis and Eduard Schaubert (the other two were Athinas St. and Piraeos St.) and today is one of the main arteries in the town. Here is found **Klauthmonas Square**.

In the neoclassical Vouros mansion, known as the Old Palace (this is where King Othon and Queen Amalia lived at the start of their reign) is housed the **Museum of Athens**. It contains exhibits that cover the history and the development of the Greek capital from the period of the Franks till the present.

Omonoia Square

Together with Syntagma Square, Omonoia is one of the largest and best known squares in Athens. The main station of the capital's metro has been operating there since the 19th century.

All the main arteries of the city either begin or end there, such as Piraeos St. (to Piraeus), Septemvriou III St. and Patission St. (to the northern suburbs and Mt. Parnitha),

and Athinas St. (to the market, Monastiraki and the Acropolis). There are many shops in Omonoia with folk articles for sale and the square itself is a meeting place. Near Omonoia are the National Theater and the **Municipal Gallery**.

Patission Street - The Pedion tou Areos

Patission St. (or 28th Oktovriou St.) starts at Omonoia. Besides the commercial shops and the civic buildings, the **National Technical School** is also here, a neoclassical building from the 19th century. There is a superb example of church architecture on Patission St., the church of Ayios Loukas (St. Luke) by the architect E. Ziller as well as the **Pedion tou Areos** (the Field of Ares) at the intersection with Alexandras Boulevard, a marvelous park which every year holds one of the largest book exhibitions in Greece.

The National Archaelogical Museum of Athens.

Exarcheia - Strefis Hill

This is one of the main squares of Athens. Bustling and full of people it has been a student hangout for many years.

Exarcheia Square, with its intense and varied night life, has a color and pulse all its own, one palpably different from the rest of the squares in the capital. There are many small tavernas, bars and outdoor summer cinemas on the narrow streets and small sidewalks around it. **Strefis Hill** rises above the square.

At its base are athletic installations and picturesque ouzo bars while at the top there is one of the finest panoramic views of Athens.

The Cultural Center of the Municipality of Athens and the statue of the great poet Kostis Palamas.

8

BYZANTINE ATHENS

Churches - Monasteries
Kaisariani Monastery - Dafni Monastery

After the division of the vast Roman empire into West and East, Athens, and Greece in general, became part of the eastern empire with its capital at ancient New Rome, that is, Constantinople. During the early Christian centuries, Athens retained strong memories of their ancient religion, reinforced by monuments. Naturally, it enjoyed the esteem and respect of the Romans and scholars but it had lost the stature and the brilliance of antiquity. After the definitive abolition of the philosophical Schools and the triumph of Christianity, churches began to be erected in Athens which were of exceptional interest for the development of art in the region. It should be noted that the number of churches that have survived, from both the Byzantine and the post-Byzantine period, is woefully small. The vicissitudes of Turkish rule as well as the

mania for the reformation of the town itself after the creation of the modern Greek state and the choosing of Athens as its eventual capital, resulted in the destruction of many monuments from that period. Those that remained were not impressive for their size but as the historian M. Chatzidakis writes concerning these the churches: "The Athenian churches should not be judged in terms of size and the baseness of the materials and thus be considered haphazard provincial monuments. Against these characteristics can be set their spiritual grace, which is shown to be pure, without the interpolation of any of the sensual delights arising from the use of luxurious materials. Because the Byzantine Athenians, faithful to their traditions, continued to love beauty, perhaps without being aware of its "unembellished nature".

Kapnikarea

Kapnikarea is dedicated to the Presentation of the Virgin Mary and is on Ermou St. near Monastiraki. It was built in the 11th century with large stones on the bottom and clay masonry higher up. It is a complex four-columned Athenian church with a single-space extension on the north side with a cupola, the chapel of Ayia Varvara (St. Barbara).

In the 12th century an outer narthex was added to the west side with a small column supporting a small outer porch.

Ayioi Apostoloi

Next to the Stoa of Attalos on a Nymphaeon from the 2nd century A.D. is the church of the Ayioi Apostoloi (the Holy Apostles).

It has well-made external masonry with large stones below and bricks above. This is an idiorrythmic inscribed cruciform church from the 10th century.

Ayios Nikolaos Rangavas

Ayios Nikolaos Rangavas (St. Nikolas Rangavas) lies beneath the Acropolis on a side street off Tripodon St. and is a building from the 11th century. It was named Rangavas after a large Byzantine family of the same name. It is a simple four-columned inscribed cruciform church.

The Russian Church

The Russian Church on Philellinon St. (near Syntagma) was formerly called the Sotiros tou Lykodimou (the Savior of Lykodimos) or the Metamorfosis tou Sotiros (the Transfiguration of the Savior). Today it is known as the church of St. Nikodimos.

It was built around 1031 by Stephanos Lykodimos. Once it was a noteworthy monastery but in 1780 the Turks destroyed it in order to use the stones to build the town wall.

Between 1852 -1856 the Savior of Lykodimos was renovated with money from the Czars Nikolaos I and Alexander II and was decorated by the German painter Thiersch.

This is an octagonal church with lavish ceramic decoration.

Ayioi Theodoroi

The Byzantine church of the Ayioi Theodoroi (The Saints Theodore) from the 11th century lies on the bottom part of Klauthmonos Square. It is a heavy structure with many archaic elements. This is an unusual variation of the cruciform church with a cupola.

Ayia Dynami

The church of Ayia Dynami (Divine Force) is overhung by the Ministry of Education on the corner of Mitropoleos and Nikis Sts.

The Divine Force was the protectress of women about to give birth. It is an estate of the Petrakis Monastery.

Ayios Andreas

Ayios Andreas (St. Andrew) is on Philothei St. behind the cathedral. The monastery of St Philothei was here. The church was erected in 1550. Here are also the relics of Saint Philothei, who founded the monastery of Ayios Andreas which was called the Parthenon of the Nuns .

Agios Eleftherios (Gorgoepikoos)

Agios Eleftherios (11th century) was the first cathedral of the new Greek state. It is next to the present-day Cathedral and was formerly called Panayia Gorgoepikoos (the Blesses Virgin Mary Who Grants Requests Swiftly).

Despite having the name of the Blessed Virgin it celebrates on Ayios Eleftherios' day because in the Greek War of Independence of 1821 the fighters gave it the name (Eleftheria = Freedom).

The first erection of the church is attributed to the woman Augousta Ireni the Athenia. (787 A.D.).

It is a type of inscribed cruiform church and it is peculiar because its exterior is completely dresses in marble plaques. 90 ancient and Byzantine scluptures have been built into it there by turning the church into a picturesque sculpture exhibit.

In 1849 it was turned into public library and in 1863 was used again as a church.

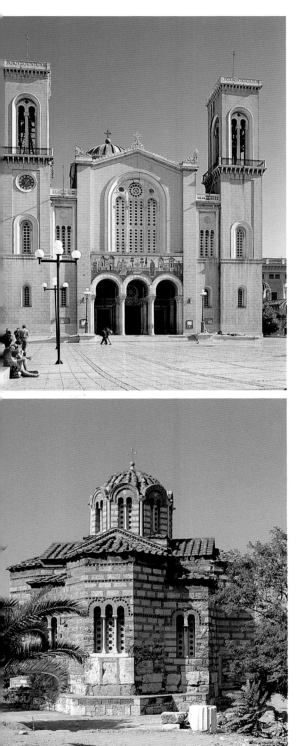

The Mitropoli (Cathedral Church)

The Cathedral Church of Athens, or the Mitropoli, is dedicated to the Annunciation and celebrates on 25 March. It is in the center of the old town of Athens, below Syntagma square to which it is connected by Mitropoleos St. It is the natural successor to the old cathedral of Ayios Eleftherios after the triumph of the Greek War of Independence and the establishment of the independent Greek state. It was founded on the 25 December 1842 by King Othon and its architect was the Bavarian Hansen, who gave the building a form that neither externally nor internally is suited to the temperament and the tradition of Greece. The wall paintings were done by Zeit, the icons on the iconostasis were made in Florence at the workshop of C. Fornelli and the holy altar door in Rome. In the basements are the side-chapels of St. Gregory V, St. Philothei and St. Skepi and a baptismal font for adults. In the main part of the church are housed the priceless relics of the Patriarch of Constantinople, Gregory V and St. Philothei the Athenian. The Cathedral of Athens, along with Ayios Eleftherios, contains features from both the glorious Byzantine past of Christianity as well as western art and thus reflects the elements that made up the Greek state in the middle of the 19th century.

Above: The present-day Cathedral of Athens, a living repository of local history.

Below: The Byzantine church of the Holy Disciples next to Stoa of Attalos.

Kaisariani Monastery

The Kaisariani Monastery lies to the rear of a shady valley with lush vegetation, at the start of the ascent of Hymettus and above the neighborhood of the same name. This superb and elegant structure was founded in the 4th or 5th century on the site of an ancient sanctuary to Aphrodite. Materials from the ancient temple were used for the first Christian church.

The present-day church was built on the old one which was destroyed in the 11th century. The various finds from the area and the Eridanos river which is near the site reveal the history of the area. It appears it was inhabited from the Mesolithic era. This is shown by tools and obsidian blades that were found there. Manolis Chatzidakis writes of the church:

"The church is more or less contemporary with Dafni, from the end of the 11th century, but built in another style, with a totally different expression. It is cruciform with a cupola supported on four columns and the proportions are narrow and high so that the dome, also narrow, is not entirely visible except when standing directly beneath it. Externally, the most beautiful side of the church is, as always, the eastern one. The vertical element is dominant here as well.

The surfaces are bare, unadorned, and unbroken by any serrated lines or friezes. The only decoration on the windows are the wavy lines of the bricks. The masses, with a clear and abrupt outline, ascend undisturbed, steady, powerful in their strict composition, practically geometrical in style. The cupola expresses the same spirit with little columns and arches for the crowning of the horizontal roof. These spare surfaces warm the faultless and yet free structure of the wall."

The monastery spring still has water. A fountain, that once had abundant water from Kalopoula, was a miracle-working spring for sterile women as well as pregnant ones. The buildings that make up the monastery are the church of the Eisodion tis Theotokou (The Presentation of the Virgin Mary), one of the most elegant Byzantine churches of Athens, and the small church of Ayios Antonios (St. Anthony) wedged in beside it.

The wall paintings in the churches of the Presentation and St. Anthony were done in 1682 by the painter Ioannis Ypatos the Peloponnesian and funded by Benizelos; they reflect the models of the Cretan School. Other interesting structures are the kitchen the refectory, the cells, the olive press, the storerooms and the marvelous fountain with its ancient ram's head. The cells of the monks were in the destroyed three-storey building (two floors survive), in the south section of the monastery. The Tower of Benizelos is to be found in the middle of the cells and is where St. Philothei lived as a nun. She was the daughter of Benizelos. After the Turkish occupation the monastery was refounded and functioned as a convent. Today it is an archaeological site, one of the gems of Athens.

Above: The Kaisariani Monastery from the 11th century.

Right page: View of the entrance to the monastery.

Dafni Monastery

"Lady of Dafni all gold
great is your charm
with your mosaics
and precious pearls."

These lines reflect the impression that was
created by the marvellous mosaics on a gold
background that decorated the interior of the
unique, from every point of view, main church of
the Monastery of the Koimisis tis Theotokou
(The Dormition of the Virgin) at Dafni,
10 kilometers outside Athens at the intersection
of the Sacred Way and the National Road to
Corinth. The monastery was originally founded
in the 5th-6th century.
The present-day Dafni Monastery is a building
from the 11th century which was built on the site
of the ancient temple of the "Laurel-Wreathed"
Apollo in the form of a complex octagonal
church. The mosaics in the church with their
gold background and particularly the Christ
Pantokrator in the dome with his stern visage
(see photo, page 96) are unique in their power
of expression and are considered to be
masterpieces of Byzantine art, some of the most
beautiful in Greece.
The Panayia Dafniotissa (Our Lady of Dafne)
is built in this enclosure which after the temple
of Apollo was home to another Early Christian
church. It was the largest church in the area with
the most lavish decoration, with multicolored
flagging, upright marble slabs on the wall and
magnificent mosaics.
In the church enclosure are various buildings,
cells, galleries, the ruins of the foundations
of the monastery's refectory and a gallery that
was added by the Franks. There are also two
sarcophagi in the enclosure, decorated with
fleur-de-lis. In the area next to the monastery a
wine festival is held every summer and attracts
thousands of Greek and foreign visitors.

Views of the fortification and the interior
of the historic Dafne Monastery from the 11th century.

CULTURE &

Athens, Piraeus, and the whole of Attica in fact, are perhaps the only inhabited areas in the world to have imbued their residents with such an overwhelming and lasting commitment to creation, thought and culture. Thousands of years have been spent in the discussion of values and the investigation of nature and mankind, and all the bloody wars that were fought to protect the rights of these free thinking people; all of this has resulted in the modern Athenian who must now further the brilliant course of his country in the development of human civilization. The modern city that today fills the Attica basin has two aspects, so very different from one another yet at the same time so closely connected: on the one hand, Athens is just another metropolis of the western world but on the other, there is this aforementioned optimism, high spirits and romanticism that define the Greek. The contemporary pace of life may be steadily eroding the force of these traditions and customs that formerly were the essence of daily life, but it has not eradicated the love and nostalgia Greeks feel for the beauty of former times. It would be difficult to find another city in the world with more groups and organizations dedicated to the investigation, preservation and promotion of dance, music, customs and roots.

Athens is one of the most important vehicles of Greek culture. Even artists from other countries, foreign communities and embassies, are to be found here, for since early in its history Athens has respected cultural differences and foreign civilizations, and thus they find it fertile ground for the cultivation of their cultural and other distinctive characteristics.

Festivals, events, exhibitions, and in general all the activities that are carried out near the sacred rock of the Acropolis, are blessed with the preconditions for success perhaps more than anywhere else.

TRADITION

The present town of Athens began to develop after the liberation of Greece and the founding of the modern Greek state, when it was made the capital of the country containing the Palace of the King (the site of the present-day parliament), the Parliament, the University, and the embassies of foreign countries as well as the new harbor at Piraeus; it became the focal point of the country's political, economic and intellectual activities.

Its development was rapid but the Balkan Wars, and the Asia Minor Disaster with the resulting hundreds of thousands of refugees, and then the Second World War interrupted this course of development.

In particular the wave of urbanization that struck the city after the ravaging of the Greek countryside by the Nazis in retaliation for the Greek Resistance, was the second powerful blow dealt its social fabric.

The political instability that followed during the period of the Greek civil war, and which reached its peak with the military coup in 1967, brought even more inhabitants of the Greek countryside into the Attica basin so that today the city numbers more than four million.

Within this city and despite all the adversities of the period, modern Athenians, with a passion reminiscent of their ancestors, have added their own creations to the spiritual wealth of Greece.

Prose and **Poetry** have always deeply affected the Greeks. In Athens, both the well-known foreign writers and the dozens of great Greek writers such as Kazantzakis, Cavafy and Elytis, as well as all the new writers and poets, continue to attract people with their work.

This love of the word, whether in prose or in poetry, has for thousands of years now made the Athenians lovers of **Philosophy**, the absolute expression of the rational quest for Truth.

The **Theater** in Athens is not merely another form of artistic creation. This city, that gave birth to contemporary western theater, has today more theaters than any other capital city, and they are always full. Most neighborhoods have their own theaters and present well-attended performances ranging from the classical repertoire to experimental and avant garde productions, as well as ballet and dance.

The **Greek Cinema**, which has produced a great number of important works of all kinds throughout its history, appears at the end of the 20th century to have taken a more poetic turn, difficult perhaps at times, which has also achieved great success such as in the works of Th. Angelopoulos,
who is perhaps the best known Greek director abroad. **Music** and **Song** are not only interesting pastimes for Greeks, but something that springs from deep within.
Greek popular music, famous throughout the world, is to be found everywhere in the city, from the radio stations to the night clubs, songs about love, and about all the good and bad times the Greeks have experienced, with a sound that is an intense mixture of western methodology and eastern scales.
So-called western music is also represented in Athens with important musicians such as Manos. Chatzidakis and M. Theodorakis, and Maria Callas in the past, and Vangelis Papathanasiou, Agni Baltsa and L. Kavakos today, who all ornament the musical landscape of Attica just as worthily as the ancient greats, the descendants of Orpheus.

This love for the word, the harmony of musicand the expressivity of the song, are perhaps the most important elements which inspire the artists in the plastic arts. Along with such stimuli and the restlessness of daily life, it gives them the cultivation to comport themselves as the descendants of Phidias or Praxiteles, or painters worthy of Nikias and architects the like of Iktinos, Kallikrates and Mnisiklis. The quality of modern Greek **Sculpture** has been internationally recognized and ornaments the town in the best of ways as there is more and more sculpture to be found in the public parts of the city, while buildings that are veritable works of art, are being erected ever more frequently by daring and inspired Greek architects. In ancient Greece, the plastic arts included **Pottery**, whose highest expression was found in the Attic pots.
But the changes brought about by contemporary life have weakened it so that after thousands of years only a few true creators are left in this field to carry on and create works of art with clay, color and inspiration.

The modern metropolis in the Attica basin has not been able to retain its **traditions** and **customs** inviolate. But there are state organizations and other private associations who come from other areas of Greece as well as from the Greek enclaves in the Balkans and Asia Minor, who have contributed highly important work related to the study of the folklore in Attica and other Greek regions. Characteristic of this are the **traditional costumes** which have been preserved, or even recreated, using time-honored means such as the loom.

Their variety and their beauty is enchanting, not to mention the marks of history shown in their decoration, with the ancient meander motifs, and Byzantine eagles, elements so closely interwoven with the course of Hellenism. An important contribution to the study of Greek attire in Attica and the rest of Greece has been made by the Dora Stratou Dance Theater in Plaka, which has collected costumes from all over Greece as well as from the Greek areas of the Balkans and Asia Minor.

But the **age old manners** and **customs** are still alive in Attica, based by and large on the Greek Orthodox Christian tradition.

The Resurrection is the greatest celebration of the Orthodox faith.

On **Holy Saturday**, millions of Christians in Athens fill the churches and the streets. Easter Sunday is a most festive day, with high spirits, music and singing.

But the other **festivals and fairs**, which are to be found primarily in the outlying districts of the capital, are also an opportunity for the visitor to experience the old beauty of the area. Thus, in Autumn, during the grape harvest there are wine festivals with dancing, music and song.

Finally, Athens has many marvelous images to offer one at **Carnival,** when Plaka and Monastiraki are filled with masqueraders.

A very moving image is also presented by all the people who have kept up the **old professions**, such as the cobbler, the blacksmith, and the instrument maker. These colorful and romantic people are yet another priceless ornament of Athens and Attica.

The history and traditions that have been brought to the city by the inhabitants of all the Greek areas, the site itself and above all Greek civilization, are the cornerstones on which the modern Athenian is based.
On the surface he is no different than the inhabitant of any other large European city, both in terms of the pace of his life and his work as well as all the daily anxiety of traffic and the consumer society. But he has managed to hold on to the ancient Greek high spirits, which led his forbearers to Dionysian revelries, as well as the optimism that the blue sky of Attica eternally inspires. He has the best time that he possibly can which is why the **night-life of Athens** is rivalled by very few of the capitals of Europe ending only at the dawn of a new day.
The crowds of people on the streets of Athens having a good time all night long and filling the city with activity, are the best proof of the real, inner beauty of its inhabitants. **Romance** is yet another aspect of the Athenian character. The unique open-air summer cinemas set amid greenery, with the light of the moon highlighting the screen, the regular exodus to the countryside and nature, for holidays and the weekend, and the unique sunsets seen from the Acropolis, are elements that are indissolubly linked to the life of every inhabitant of Attica. The **tavernas, cafes, shops**, and the **concert halls**, are full every day, and they liberate the Athenian from the isolation, monotony and fatiguing pace of our contemporary life.
Greeks are famous for their passion and the Athenians are no exception. **Athletics,** social events, and politics are always an occasion for having a good time or discussions to the point of exhaustion. This is also an important proof of the vitality, the intense interest and the speculative mind which have always nourished the inhabitants of the capital and kept them involved with what is going on around them, in distinction to the inhabitants of other large cities in Europe.

The center and the neighborhoods of Athens which existed before the middle of the 20th century are what attract the visitor's eye with their beautiful neoclassical buildings, their baroque mansions and their austere public buildings, and these have remained to beautify areas which in the difficult decades after the end of World War II experienced anarchic growth in its most virulent form.

But throughout the city there is a steady increase of modern and aesthetically daring buildings while new ornaments such as the **Music Megaron** make Athens even more beautiful. The city of Athens is today spread over the entire basin and continues to steadily advance to the east and north, as both the

Municipality of Athens and the other municipalities in the basin continue to bring to realization the upgrading of the present center, with a corresponding reduction of the number of its inhabitants. Moreover, the city's new Metro and the rapidly improving means of mass transport make it much easier to reach the suburbs of Athens, which relieves the center of its heavy burden of traffic. The Municipality of Athens has already offered the many works which are daily helping to beautify the city that inaugurated beauty of the spirit and harmony to the world.

The Auditorium of the Friends of Music of the Athens Music Megaron, one of the finest concert halls in the entire world.

The Museums of Athens

The Archaeological Museum

The National Archaeological Museum is housed in a two-storey neoclassical building that was built to the specifications of Lange, with modifications by Ziller, from 1866-1898 and it is located on Patission Street 44, at the corner of Tositsa Street. It has on display finds from all parts of the ancient Greek world dating from the Neolithic period until the end of the Roman empire. This is the richest and most important museum in the world in terms of ancient Greek art. Today the National Archaeological Museum has one of the most lavish collections in existence of the sculpture and pottery of Greece during Archaic, Classical and Hellenistic times. While one is admiring them it is also worthwhile examining the equally marvellous finds from the Neolithic, Cycladic and Mycenean periods.

Above: The famous Cycladic figurine of the Harp-Player.
Below: The Knowned "Jockey", a sculptural complex consisting of an horse and young rider.

In **room 4** are exhibited antiquities from 1800-1100 B.C. which come from the houses, tombs and palaces of Mycenae, Tiryns, Argos and Attica.

The "Mask of Agamemnon",
from the royal Tholos tombs of Argos.

In **room 5** are housed stone and ceramic objects from the Neolithic period and the Bronze Age and in **room 6** objects of prehistoric Cycladic art are on display. In **room 7** one finds pottery and sculpture from Geometric and Archaic times and there is a statue of the goddess Artemis from Delos, circa 650 B.C. In **room 8** the colossal Kouros from Sounion stands out and in **room 9** there are several magnificent sculptures from the middle of the 6th century B.C. such as the statue of a winged victory (Nike). In r**ooms 10 and 11** is to be found sculpture from the 6th century B.C. In rooms **12 and 13** the exhibition of sculpture from the 6th century B.C. continues and includes the marvellous Kouros of Anavyssos. In **room 14** the "Self-Crowning Ephebe" from Sounion (400 B.C.) is worthy of note and in **room 15** the bronze statue of Poseidon or Zeus Artemisios. In rooms **16-28** the art of Classical times unfolds through sculpture and funerary reliefs.

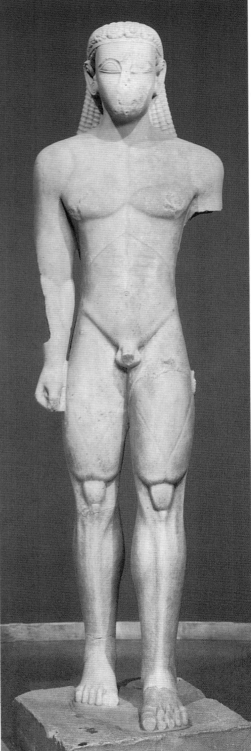

The famed Archaic Kouros of Sounion.

The "Ephebe of Antikythera.

Marble sculptural group of Aphrodite, Pan and the small Eros.

In **rooms 29 and 30** Hellenistic sculpture is on display. The Ephebe of Antikythera is exceptional, as well as the statues of Poseidon and Themis. In **room 32** is to be found the collection of Eleni Stathatos and in **rooms 36-37** the Karapanos collection containing mainly bronze objects from the Oracle of Zeus at Dodoni.

In **rooms 41, 42, 43** can be seen marble and bronze Roman sculpture, portraits of Roman emperors and Herm steles of Greek luminaries. In **room 48** are displayed the finds discovered in the excavations on Santorini. Of particular interest are the pots made with a local technique. But the exceptional wall paintings of the Minoan painters on the island are what steals one's interest while giving us valuable information on the daily life of Santorini in the 16th century B.C.,

before the volcanic eruption. **Room 49** contains ceramics from the Bronze Age to the Geometric period, **room 50** contains Geometric and Orientalizing ceramics and **room 51** has pottery in the so-called Proto-Attican style. **Rooms 52 and 53** contain black-figured pottery from the 7th to the 6th century B.C. which come mainly from Attican workshops and in **room 54** there is both black-figured and red-figured pottery.

The red-figured krater from the Acropolis, by the Seriskos Painter is worth particular attention.

In **room 55** the collection of white lekythes are sure to attract one's interest. These were special vases used in funeral ceremonies and finally in **room 56** there are red-figured pots from the end of the 5th and the 4th century B.C.

Of especial note are the six Panathanaic amphoras, black-figured vases that were found on the ancient way to Eretria.

The National Archaeological Museum also houses a **Numismatic Collection**. This is one of the most important collections of its kind in the world. It contains many rare Greek coins from the 7th century B.C. until the modern period, from Roman, Byzantine, medieval, and the recent past as well as modern Greek and foreign coins. It also has a collection of lead-seals, bronze and lead Archaic symbols, Archaic and Byzantine measures, and stone sculpture. **Inscription Collection**. It contains over 13,000 inscriptions from the 6th century B.C, until 300 A.D. On display are inscriptions of highly important historical, religious or philosophical value as well as the bases of works of art with the names of great artists on them. **Santorini Exhibition**. All the finds from the ancient town on Santorini are on display. **Museum Reproductions**. In the National Archaeological Museum there is a shop where reproductions of the various statues and other artifacts in Greek museums are for sale, all with an official certificates of authenticity.

Wall paintings from the excavations on the Cycladic town of Akrotiri, Santorini, above the "Fisherman" and below details from the large wall paintings with depictions of ships.

The Byzantine Museum

The Byzantine Museum (V. Sofias Ave. 22) is housed in the mansion of the Duchess of Piacenza which was built in 1848 in the style of a Florentine Palace by the great Greek architect S. Kleanthis. It is the largest and most important museum in the country for Byzantine art and contains many noteworthy Early Christian, Byzantine and Frankish sculptures and architectural members. Entire churches, including a triple-aisled basilica, a cruciform church with dome and a post-Byzantine church have been reconstructed inside the museum. It has splendid collections of Byzantine and post-Byzantine icons, detached wall paintings and Byzantine manuscripts. There are also the finest ecclesiastical embroideries, vessels and jewellery, as well as wood carvings, ceramics and various small objects.

Above: The Virgin Mary and the infant Jesus, 15th century.
Below: "The Hospitality of Abraham", 15th century.

The Benaki Museum

This museum is housed in the old neoclassical mansion of Emmanuel Benakis (V. Sofias & Koumbari 1). It consists of the many personal collections of Antonis Benakis and has been enriched by numerous subsequent additions. The museum has on display lavish and important collections of Greek art from the prehistoric period to modern times, ancient ceramics, bronze and above all gold jewellery. There are also Byzantine and post-Byzantine icons, manuscripts, incredible ecclesiastical embroideries, religious vessels, jewellery and wood carvings. In addition there are superb collections of local costumes, embroideries, jewellery, metalworking, and wood-carving, and weapons; relics, historical mementos, water colors and lithographs are also to be found.

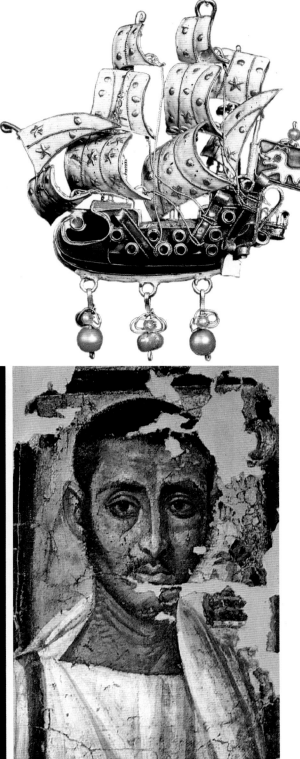

Above: gold jewellery.

Below: Geometric amphora with representations and the death mask of a young man from Fayyum.

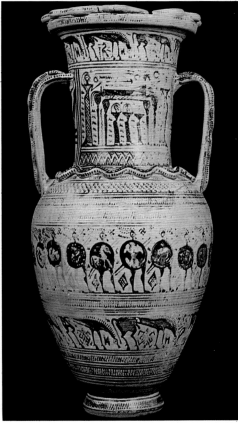

The Kanellopoulos Museum

The exhibits in the Kanellopoulos Museum
(Thereias St., right below the Acropolis) reflect
two periods: late pagan and early Christian.
One of the interesting groups found in the
museum is the Tanagra figurines, miniature clay
figures with female forms.
The Tanagra figurines were found in the ancient
town of Tanagra and belong to the period
330-200 B.C. The museum is housed in a
neoclassical mansion from the end of the 19th
century where the personal collection of the P.
and A. Kanellopoulos is displayed in the most
appropriate manner.

The Ethnological and Historical Museum

This museum is housed in the Old Parliament
building on Stadiou Street which was built
in 1858 to the plans of Boulanger. It contains
valuable artifacts and mementos of the nation's
struggles, and paintings, engravings and
sculpture. There are also documents, seals,
and military keepsakes from the Byzantine
period, local costumes, embroideries,
wood carvings, ceramics, metal objects
and other works of folk art.

The War Museum

The military remnants and mementos of Greece
from the Neolithic period to the present have
been gathered here. The museum is located on
the corner of Vas. Sofias Avenue and Rizari St.

The Sculpture in the 1st Cemetery

The 1st Cemetery of Athens, which lies
northeast of the columns of Olympian Zeus,
is an open-air sculpture gallery, with works
of the great sculptors of modern Greece.

Other Museums

During our tour of the city of Athens we have
come to know, besides the Acropolis
Museum, many other smaller museums such
as the Museum of Athens in Klathmonos
Square, the Museum of Cycladic Art in
Kolonaki, the Education Museum in Plaka,
the Museum of the Ancient Agora, and the
Kerameikos Museum.

One of the amazing works by Domenico Theotokopoulos (El Greco), "The Concert of Angels" (National Gallery of Greece).

The National Gallery

The National Gallery-Alexandros Soutzos Museum lies at the junction of Vasileos Konstantinou Avenue and Michalakopoulou St. The installations were completed in two successive stages in 1964 and 1976 based on the plans of the architects P. Mylonas, D. Fatouros and D. Antonakakis. With approximately 20,000 works of painting, sculpture, engraving, drawing, and valuable miniatures and furniture from various periods, it is the only Museum of the History of Art in Greece. Besides important icons from the Cretan School it also houses portraits from the Ionian Island School of the 18th-19th century as well as works with subjects taken from the Greek War of Independence of 1821. The early years after Greek independence was achieved are represented by the works of the Greek painters G. and Ph. Margaritis, A. Kriezis, Ph. Pitse, V. Landza, A. Oikonomou, N. Kounelakis and continues on with the works of Th. Vryzakis, N. Lytras, N. Gysis, G. Iakovidis, S. Savvidis and K. Volonakis, painters who studied in Munich and introduced western European painting into Greece for the first time but employing subjects which were connected to their country's historical environment.

Sculpture from the 19th century is represented by P. Prosalentis, L. and G. Fytalis, D. Philippotis, G. Vroutos, and L. Drosos while from the 20th

century there are Y. Chalepas, A. Sochos, Dimitriadis, G. Zongolopoulos, Th. Apartis, M. Makris, Takis, Chryssa, Ph. Eythymiadis-Menegakis, G. Sklavos, Y. Parmakellis and K. Kouletianos. The 20th century is also represented by works of important Greek painters who in seeking an identity for the modern Greek nation created new symbols through the use of new techniques and images. They belong to the so-called "heroic" generation and include Y. Moralis, G. Gaïtis, P. Tetsis, K. Xenakis, and A. Fasianos all modern classics. From the rich collection of western European painting we mention the "Concert of Angels"by Domenico Theotokopoulos (El Greco), the "Crucifixion" by Lorenzo Veneziano, "The Instrument-Maker" by Cecco del Caravaggio, "Eliezar and Rebecca" by G. B. Tiepolo, and "The Table of Lights" by J. Jordaens. In 1995 the purchase of "St. Peter" by El Greco was completed. In the important engraving collection can be found series of woodcuts and copperplates. The history of Greek engraving is fully represented throughout its whole extent. The National Gallery has made it a matter of policy to present exhibitions from time to time in specially constructed spaces which are concerned with important Greek or pictorial exhibitions from abroad, done in cooperation with private collections and foreign museums.

The Attica basin, where ancient Athens was born and grew to greatness, is also the home of the modern city which is defined by an arc of mountain masses, the only open side being to the south facing the sea. Construction is already climbing the lower and the upper slopes of the mountains, and there is continual development, with the creation of new neighborhoods and autonomous administrative municipalities around the center of the town.

Hymettus hosts along its lower slopes the eastern suburbs which are Argyroupoli, Ilioupoli, Vyronas, Zographos, Kaisariani, Ayia Paraskevi and many other neighborhoods, most of them in the basin itself.

Penteli has the northern suburbs on both its lower and higher southwestern slopes: Psychiko, Philothei, Chalandri, Marousi and Kifissia and higher up Vrilissia and Palaia and Nea Penteli are areas that are both green and have a modern street-plan.

Parnitha, to the northwest, is the site of Menidi and Thrakomakedones, nestled deep in verdant nature.

Aigaleo, from where Xerxes watched the naval battle of Salamis and the defeat of his fleet in 480 B.C., plays host to the western suburbs : Liosia, Peristeri, Aigaleo, Chaldari, Nikaia, Korydallos, Keratsini which are some of the most heavily populated areas of Athens and Piraeus.

Moni Pentelis.

suburbs and surrounding mountains

Penteli

Despite the great destruction done by the quarries and fire, Penteli still is a place near the capital where one can enjoy a stroll through nature. On Penteli are found the famous quarries of white marble which were used in antiquity for the building and the carving of all the treasures of Athens.

*The **northern suburbs** are what the areas on the southwest slopes of Penteli are called and you reach them by following Kifissias Avenue from Ambelokipi Square. After Psychiko, Philothei and Chalandri you reach Maroussi.*

Maroussi - Kifissia

Maroussi *is the ancient Athmonon with the sanctuary of Amarysia Artemis. Ancient inscriptions and tombs have been found there. The Byzantine church of the Panayia Neratziotissa (The Virgin Mary of the Bitter Oranges) next to the train lines is a real jewel. The installations for the **Olympic Stadium** and the Olympic Village, large hospitals and OTE (The Phone Company) are all found in Maroussi.*

The Ceramic Exhibition:
the permanent exhibition showroom for all the potters in Greece is located there.

Pefki *and then **Kifissia** lie above Maroussi. Kifissia is a much frequented and well-liked suburb in this part of the capital and the terminus of the electric train which comes from Piraeus. It is a living flower garden with beautiful neighborhoods such as Kefalari and Politeia. Kifissia lies on the site of the ancient deme of the Erechtheis. The comic poet Menandros, who wrote 108 comedies, was born there (342 B.C.)*

Herod Atticus (101-177 A.D.) also lived in Kifissia. He had a magnificent villa where the Cathedral church is today.

The Museum of Natural History:
The Museum of Natural History (Goulandris) is located in Kifissia and has a wealth of exhibits. It is both a museum and a research center on the Greek fauna, flora, geology and paleontology.

Ekali - Dionysos - Drosia

After Kifissia comes **Nea Erythraia** and then **Ekali** at the 20th kilometer. This suburb has a great number of villas and verdant gardens. Ekali took its name from the woman who provided Theseus with hospitality when he went to kill the bull that was ravaging the plain of Marathon. Returning in triumph, Theseus established a festival in the district in honor of Ekaleios Zeus. From Ekali the road to the right goes up to **Dionysos**, at the site of Ayios Petros, with a splendid view of the Gulf of Euboea and then descends to Nea Makri and Marathon (p. 146). It is the same road that existed in antiquity, the one that joined Ekali to the Tetrapoli of Marathon. The Athenian forces passed through here in 490 B.C. on their way to take part in the victorious battle against the Persians at Marathon.

At Dionysos there is the archaeological site of ancient Ikaria, a very old center for the worship of the god Dionysos. The poet Thespis, who laid the basis for ancient drama, also came from this district. Here were found the ancient theater, a sanctuary to the god, ruins of the temple of Pythia Apollo, sacred buildings and the base of a choregic monument. After Ekali come **Drosia, Stamata, Bala** and **Kryoneri.**

Above: The ultramodern facilities of the Olympic Center of Athens, one of the finest in Europe with the largest enclosed playing field on the continent (20,000 spectators).

Center: Park of Kifissia.

Below: The Goulandris Museum of Natural History, one of the more important places to visit in Kifissia and Athens.

The Penteli Monastery

In antiquity Penteli was called Vrilissos and during the Middle Ages "the mountain of the blameless" in reference to the many monks who had taken refuge there. After Chalandari and Vrilissia you reach the square of Palaia Penteli with its small picturesque church of Ayia Triada (Holy Trinity). Further up, on the left, is Penteli Monastery. Bishop Timotheos arrived there from Euboea in 1575 and built the monastery. It is a typical monastery from the post-Byzantine period with a main church dedicated to the Panayia (The Virgin Mary). The monastery's Old Peoples Home has been turned into a museum. In the underground spaces (catacombs) of the monastery is housed the Museum of the Orthodox Greek Clergy and Greek Education during the time of the Turkish occupation.

In one rectangular underground space, 4x6 m., there is a reproduction of a Secret School , based on the painting of the great Greek painter Nikiphoros Lytras.

In the labyrinthian underground pathways and corners one finds the Permanent Exhibition of the Holy Scripture. Here various icons are on display which bring the pages of the Old and New Testaments to life.Penteli Monastery -- in the building complex that makes up the Orthodox Center --also houses the Foundation of Byzantine Musicology. There is a reading room, a library and administrative offices.

It has been endowed with many musical manuscripts of great value.

There is a microfilm library and audio studios. Next to the Penteli Monastery a road begins which ends at the **Davelis Cave** in the area of the ancient quarries, at an altitude of 720 m. The cave was made during antiquity when the entire surrounding region was a quarry from which the marble for the Acropolis was cut. On the eastern side of the cave is the chapel of Ayios Nikolaos (St. Nicholas) from the 11th century and the hermitage of Ayios Spyridonas (St. Spyridon). Marvelous wall paintings have survived in the chapels in the cave. The most important ones are in the dome of St. Nikolas.

Parnitha

Mt. Parnitha is the highest of the mountains that rim Athens (1,413 m.). At one thousand and ten meters is the Monastery of Ayia Triada (the Holy Trinity), the spring and the bus terminus. Despite its many turns it is a good automobile road.

You can go up Parnitha on a funicular railway which starts at the sight called Metochi (22 km.) and reaches the hotel and casino.

The road from **Nea Philadelphia, Kokkinos Mylos** and **Lykotrypa** goes to **Acharnes.**

From Acharnes (Menidi) the road goes up to 1,010 m. There is a refuge of the Mountain Climbing Association on Mt. Parntha. At a distance of 7 km. from here is the Mola Spring. Nearby is the church of Ayios Petros (St. Peter) with one cell for the convenience of passing mountain climbers, hunters and lumberjacks. West of the Holy Trinity is Palaiochori with the skiing installations of EOS (Mountain Climbing Association).

Even further west is the National Forest of Parnitha which has wild animals. At the sight called Bafi, at 1,165 m., is the up-to-date refuge of the Mountain Climbing Association suitable for 100 climbers.

Acharnes

Ancient Menidi, or Acharnes, was the largest of the ten demes of ancient Attica which were set up in compliance with the reforms instituted by Kleisthenis.

The ruins that were found on the hill of Profitis Ilias consisted of an amphitheater, an ancient inscription in marble, many pots and statues, an aqueduct and Mycenean offerings in a tholos tomb.

Fyli

On the slopes of Parnitha, 16 km. from Athens, is the village of **Hasia or Fyli** with its many tavernas. To the right on the mountain itself is the new **Monastery of Ayios Kyprianos** (St. Cyprian). **Moni Kleiston** (Kleiston Monastery) is another monastery at Hasia located on a captivating site just outside the village.

Moni Kleiston is a monastery from the 14th century built on a rock on the edge of a ravine through which the Goura stream rushes. The main church of the monastery, built into the rock, is in the Byzantine style and has wall paintings.

The region around the monastery is enchanting. Sunday morning many worshippers gather there. A natural cave was discovered on the slopes of the ravine of Goura dedicated to the worship of Pan and the Nymphs.

Three kilometers after Hasia the road (before Moni Kleiston) branches to the left and then becomes passable only on foot. At an altitude of 683 m. you reach the garrison of Fyli which was a natural fortification for the mountain approaches to Attica and Athens. The garrison has quite marvellous ashlar masonry with both square and round towers. Fyli is an example of the old systematic fortifications which employed reinforced bastions.

Hymettus

Prokris, the daughter of Erechtheas, along with her husband Kefalos, roamed the ravines, gorges and springs of Hymettus hunting. Near Kallia Pigi, Kefalos killed his wife by accident. At this site there was a temple to Aphrodite in antiquity and was called Kyllos Pira, the present-day Kalopoula.

During early Christian years a church was built on this holy site with pieces of marble from the ancient temple. Another Christian church was later built on its ruins which took the name Kaisariani. A short way above the Monastery of Kaisariani (see page 100) and at Kalopoula is one of the most elegant temples on the mountains of Attica, the Asteri Temple. Now renovated, it is one of the most beautiful settings for a stroll.

Kareas Monastery

On the slopes of Hymettus, the
Monastery of Kaisariani, is the
post-Byzantine monastery
of Ayios Ioannis Prodromos
(St. John the Baptist), the so-called
Karea, on a beautiful site.
There is an Early Christian funerary
plaque on the floor of the monastery
church. Both this Early Christian
plaque and the ancient and Byzantine
pieces of sculpture with which **Karea**
was decorated, make it clear there
was an even older monastery here.

*Views of the post-Byzantine Kareas Monastery on
the slopes of Mt. Hymettus.*

PIRAEUS

Climbing the Acropolis and looking toward the sea, the town can be seen stretching all the way to the shores of Attica,
where Piraeus lies, the largest harbor in the Balkans and one of the largest in the Mediterranean.

Even today when both towns have become one ekistic unit Piraeus has kept its own personality and its own special character which has made it beautiful from antiquity right up to the present. Its three harbors played host to the Athenian ships which travelled throughout the Mediterranean and even further, transporting Greek culture and introducing new ideas and arts so that the miracle of the Golden Age could come into being.

But even today it remains one of the main routes from Europe to Asia and Africa, a bustling crossroads of people and cultures. The modern town of Piraeus was created during the more general recreation of the Greek state, as the harbor for the capital. The buildings that have survived from that period bear witness to untrammelled development, both economic and intellectual. This optimism and creativity was the reason why the town could stand up to the enormous blows inflicted by the hundreds of thousands of refugees from Asia Minor in 1922 and the terrible destruction during the Second World War.

Thus today Piraeus is the home base of Greek shipping, the largest commercial fleet in the world, a space bound to the sea like few others. The harbors of Zea and Mikrolimano as well as Phaliro play host to countless yachts and sailing craft throughout the year and all the area's night-life is concentrated along the shores of the Saronic Gulf which has inspired the inhabitants of Piraeus for thousands of years.

he Porto Leone of the Mediterranean

Piraeus has been inhabited since prehistoric times. The settlement of Mounichia (the present-day Kastella) was created then. Themistocles, a Greek political genius, later thought of utilizing this large natural harbor. He correctly noted the advantageous position of the three bays -- the large harbor, Zea (the present-day Pasalimani) and Mounichia (the present-day Mikrolimano) -- and convinced the Athenians to transfer their port from Phaliron to Piraeus, the settlement of the shipbuilders.

Foreseeing a new attack by the Persians-- after the battle of Marathon - he built in 487-486 B.C. large fortification works and thus made it into a military harbor.

The shipyards that were created then built the mighty Athenian fleet which distinguished itself at the battle of Salamis.

The fortifications of Themistocles were completed by Kimon and Pericles with the construction of the Long Wall, by which Athens and Piraeus were joined. Its construction was completed in 456 B.C. by Pericles.

During its peak period the harbor of Piraeus contained 372 "neosoikoi" (sheds near the sea where ships were kept when they were not at sea), "skeuothikes" (the yards for the rigging of warships) and shipyards for the building of ships. The area was a war zone and entrance was forbidden to private parties.

The particular importance that Piraeus had for the city-state of Athens was appreciated by Pericles and he created a number of innovative works in the city. To Hippodamos, the town planner and architect, is owed the layout, the buildings and the sacred theaters that were built. The main agora was named in his honor. Piraeus, as a port, would follow the fate of Athens. Thus, after the end of the Peloponnesian Wars when Athens came under Spartan occupation , Piraeus was to bear the brunt of the victors' rage.

The walls would be torn down, the triremes found in the harbor surrendered to the Spartans or burned, while the renowned neosoikoi would be pulled down and indeed in an almost festive manner -- with music, dancing and songs.

After the reinstatement of democracy, Konon would rebuild the walls (393 B.C.), would fund the temples of Aphrodite Euploia, the sanctuary of Zeus Sotiros and Athena and would build the famous Skeuothiki of Philon the ruins of which were discovered at Pasalimani. This revival of the town was quashed by the Roman Sylla who destroyed Piraeus. His work was completed in 395 A.D. by the Goths under Alaric.

During the Byzantine period the harbor of Piraeus was used at various intervals, but it was very far from the capital, Constantinople.

During the Turkish occupation, Piraeus was deserted. There was only the Customs house and the monastery of St. Spyridonas.

Of the old glory of the harbor there was only one marble lion left at its entrance (which is also why the area was then called Porto Leone), but unfortunately it was taken by the Venetian Morosini in 1688 as a memento of his campaign against the Turks. Today it can be found at the Naval Station of Venice and its return to its homeland is the dream of all the inhabitants of Piraeus. With the liberation of the Greek state and the proclamation of Athens as the capital, the port again acquired a reason for existence and growth and was to develop into a great commercial and industrial center.

It would be called the Manchester of the East. The town flourished and lovely buildings were constructed. One of them, which continues to ornament the present town, is the Municipal Theater, an example of neoclassical architecture of which little is left in the Balkans. Furthermore, the industrial buildings with which Piraeus is filled make for a true museum of industrial architecture. One should note the Dilaveri factory which was utilized by local authorities and the DEH (Public Power Corporation) plant which has been converted into a museum. Today Piraeus is the largest port in the Balkans and buzzes with life.

Above:The Metropolitan church of the Holy Trinity in Piraeus.
Below: The copy of the lion that was taken awat by Morosini, sitting on the southern end of the end of the entrance to the harbor of Piraeus.

Tour of Piraeus

We will begin our tour of the lovely city of Piraeus at the impressive **Electric Train Station**, the starting point for every traveller who wants to get to know the town.

This building is a noteworthy example of neoclassical architecture and bears witness to the town's former glory and dominates the center of the harbor, especially in the evening when it is illuminated.

South of the train station never completed still remains a symbol of the position of Piraeus in the modern world of global shipping.

Directly across from this example of contermporary architecture is the neoclassical building housing the Bank of Greece and the **Cathedral** of the **Ayia Triada**, which is reddish in color with an exquisite dome.

Continuing your tour along the side of the harbor and after passing a small park (where there was a famous clock tower that has unfortunately been pulled down) you will pass by the church of **Ayios Spyridonas**, the oldest and most historic church in the town and then you will head for the exhibiton halls of the **Port Authority of Piraeus**, inspired by international architecture, where large commercial exhibitions are reqularly held.

Directly opposite is the church of **Ayios Nikolaos**, patron saint of sailors everywhere. You are now on **Akti Miaouli**, the main thoroughfare along the waterfront, where most of the shipping offices and agencies are located. At strategic points along this boulevand the Port Authority of Piraeus has created passenger terminals where travellers can get the information on the schedules of passenger ships and the embarkation points.

Heading toward **Akti Xaveriou**, dotted with ultramodern buildings housing the shipping companies, you will reach the end of the street and the gates of the harbour where the ancient lion of Piraeus stands quard, a copy of the original which is in Venice.

The labyrinthian shape of the coast of the Piraeus peninsula can disorient a visitor who has not studied a map of the town.

Peiraiki - Zea Harbor

Having completed your tour of the central harbor of Piraeus you will then head south traversing the peninsula and arrive at **Peiraiki** *one of the most picturesque neighborhoods in the city, perfect for a stroll, with the remnants of the long wall and old buildings which the Municipality has taken care to properly maintain. Here one finds the Piraeus that travellers spoke of at the beginning at the* **harbor of Zea,** *one of the largest marinas in the Mediterranean, with countless foreign boats, restaurants and entertainment centers. The* **Naval Museum** *(page 133) is located in Zea marina square. Continuing on your tour you enter the small bay of* **Pasalimani,** *an area containing a number of marinas which starts at* **Freatida** *and goes all the way to* **Alexandras Square**. *The entire length of the waterfront has wonderful establishments for food, ice-cream and coffe and there are entertainment centers as well. At night it seems even more luminious and magical! You can continue your tour along the waterfront heading toward Kastella but a small deviation toward the city center will be useful for then you can visit the verdant* **square of the Municipal Theater** *with cafeterias and shops of all kinds surrounding it. The magnificent building housing the* **Municipal Theater** *as well as the* **Town Hall** *and the* **Library** *complete the picture presented by the main square in the city.*

In this page: Scene from Peiraïki down to Alexandrias Square.

Right page above: The magnificent building housing the Municipal Theater of Piraeus. Below: Zea harbor (Pasalimani).

Kastella - Mikrolimano

If one had to set aside one specific part of Piraeus as being special it would, without a doubt, be **Kastella hill** or **Mikrolimano**. It is the most picturesque harbor in Piraeus and has a vitality all its qwn supplied by all the fish tavernas there, located right down on the sea and the luxury restaurants with their cosmopolitan setting. An area with its own special color and identity, an ideal place for a stroll and a meal. In Mikrolimano the villa of Alexandras Koumounduros has been refurbished and today houses the **Naval Society of Greece**.

Above: The "Votsalakia" ("Pebbles"), the lovely beach at Kastella.

Kastella is also noted for **Votsalakia beach** which has developed into a sports center and **Profitis Ilias** which has an enchanting view of the entire Saronic gulf; there is also the **Veaki outdoor Theater** which plays host to many theatrical performances and concerts during the summer months.

Below: Mikrolimano (aerial photograph).

The Archaeological Museum of Piraeus

In the **Archaeological Museum** of Piraeus (Charilaou Trikoupi St 31) are displayed noteworthy funerary reliefs from the 5th and the 4th century B.C. and Hellenistic and Roman sculptures. Also on display are ceramics from the Classical period, bronze idols, miniature objects and coins. Of particular importance are the four bronze statues among which is a unique bronze kouros.

The Naval Museum

The **Naval Museum** is located on one side of Zea. Here are exhibited models of ships, relics from naval battles and the seafaring exploits of the Greeks, paintings, porcelain, maps, drawings, historical documents, printed matter, mementos of eminent figures and photographs. This includes all the naval activity carried out during the Greek Revolution of 1821 and contemporary naval exploits achieved during World War II. There are rooms set aside for the navy in ancient Greece, the navy in Byzantium, the navy in enslaved Greece, the navy in 1821. There are also rooms for the merchant marine and the military navy.

Right page, above: The unique bronze kouros from the Archaeological Museum of Piraeus.

Below: The forecourt of Naval Museum at the port of Zea.

AKTI APOLLONA

From Phaliro to Sounion and Lavrion

Since antiquity the sea has been an indissoluble part of Greek culture. Athens and Piraeus linked their brilliant course down through the centuries with the marine element, even in mythical times. Po-seidon, the Olympian god of the sea, claimed the protection of the town and only Athena, the goddess of Wisdom and Reason, was able to defeat him. The points where the lacy shores of Attica meet and dally with the waves, is a vital zone for Athenians, even today. The area that begins at Piraeus and Palaio Phaliro and extends eastward down to the Temple of Poseidon at Sounion, is called Akti Apollona ("The Coast of Apollo"). Along it one can find some of the most modern and expensive areas in the capital, such as Glyfada and Voula. The commercial and economic activity in these areas can be compared in intensity and variety with that in the center of town while the night-life has an intensity all its own. Continuing further east, along the Saronic Gulf, you pass through highly developed tourist resort areas. Vouliagmeni, which sets an extremely high standard in its tourist installations, Varkiza, Ayia Marina, Sa-ronida, and Ana-vyssos attract a large number of tourists as well as a significant number of the residents of Athens during the summer months. The beautiful beaches and the succession of lovely little coves are ideal for swimming and marine sports. Continuing on you will come to the historical area at the Temple of Poseidon in Sounion which gazes out over the Aegean sea, the guardian of the city that has had links with the sea like few others. Finally, you arrive at Lavrio, the mining center of ancient Attica, with which ancient Athens supported itself and which today has a well-developed harbor.

On the south coast of Attica the visitor has countless choices to make. The historical monuments lie next to up-to-date beaches, the picturesque sights are almost side by side with the most well-stocked markets and tourist installations. Here is where contemporary Attica reveals its most beautiful face.

After Piraeus comes Pasalimani to the east
followed by Mikrolimano and Kastella.
Next to Kastella is Neo Phaliron. The Stadium
of Peace and Friendship, where athletic meets,
concerts and exhibitions are held, is located
there. After Moschato comes the Delta
of Phaliron and the race track. Floisvos has
areas designed for strolling, and many hotels,
discotheques, and pastry shops. Alimos
is where both airports lie. The west airport
is used by Olympic Airways, for both internal
and external flights, and the east airport for
international flights.
Akti Apollona continues: Glyfada, Voula,
Kavouri, and Vouliagmeni. Verdant seaside
suburbs full of life and with many hotels, modern
commercial centers, tavernas, discos, pubs,
luxury villas, boat clubs, schools for
water-skiing, and wind-surfing, and there
are fully-organized beaches everywhere.
Above the beach at Vouliagmeni the road leads
after a few meters to Lake Vouliagmeni.
This is a wonderful spot wedged in between
high rocks and greenery. The lake has been
fashioned into a spa with a hotel and other
appropriate installations. It has been officially
designated a therapeutic spa by the Greek
Tourist Organization.
But it is also noteworthy for its depth: there
is a fissure in one end of it of which has not yet
been fathomed and it is a pole of attraction
for the more daring.
Varkiza follows, a beautiful seaside suburb,
and then comes **Vari** with its grilled meat
tavernas, **Saronida, Anavyssos** and **Legrena**.
At the end of the drive is impressive Cape
Sounion embraced by the Aegean Sea,
with the temple of Poseidon at its highest point.

The south coast of Attica has a variety
of facilities for everyone such
as the Friendship Stadium at Faliro,
the marina at Vouliagmeni and the famed lake
in the same area while there are also the resort centers
such as the one at Varkiza with its marina.

Sounion

The area around Sounion is connected to the myth of Theseus and the Minotaur of Crete. According to myth Minos, the King of Crete, had obliged Athens to send seven young men and seven young women to him each year as a sacrifice to the Minotaur. Theseus, the son of Aegeus, the King of Athens, wanted to free his town from this blood tribute.

The ship with the young people was readied. Black sails were raised on its masts but if the venture was successful, Aegeus had requested that white sails be raised in their place. With his great strength Theseus killed the Minotaur and following the thread of Ariadne found the exit easily. But caught up in his joy he forgot to change the black sails. Thus the unfortunate Aegeus, surveying the sea from Sounion and seeing the ship coming with the black sails, thought it certain that his son was lost and leapt into the sea - and since that time it has been called the Aegean Sea!

The view of the Aegean is enchanting. For the ancient Greeks Sounion was a place of great strategic importance and in 412 B.C. large fortification works were built there at the sacred headland as the Athenians called the cape. Today the ruins of the temple of Poseidon can still be seen there. Of the entire temple 15 columns have survived which stand out impressively. There at the end of the rock. are the Kavokolones ("Mooring-rocks") as the sailors call them, because when they see them from the open sea they know they are near the harbor of Piraeus. The temple of Poseidon was built in 444-440 B.C.

The surviving carvings on the frieze depict scenes from the Battle with the Centaurs, the Battle with the Giants and the feats of Theseus. Below the temple of Poseidon are the ruins of the temple of Souniada Athena.

Sounion, the southernmost tip of Attica where the Temple to Poseidon is located.

Lavrio

Lavrio lies 9 km. from Sounion on the east coast of Attica. An industrial town with a fishing tradition, Lavrio is full of monuments from the past, both ancient and more recent. Lavriotiki, one of the richest mining and ore regions in the world, began to offer its wealth (silver, lead, with some iron and copper) to miners as far back as prehistoric times (3100-3000 B.C.).

But in the 5th and 4th century B.C. production surged and the deposits in the region were systematically extracted, bringing thousands of tons of silver and millions of tons of lead to Athens and perhaps providing the most important basis for Athenian Democracy.

From that time the mining was mainly involved with the reworking of the ancient shafts through improvements made on ancient technology until the mines were abandoned in the 6th century A.D.

The silver used in St. Sophia in Constantinople was the last hurrah of antiquity.

The area would remain deserted until the middle of the 19th century when the industrial exploitation of the ancient rubbish was undertaken anew, and this lasted until 1989. But Lavrio has also developed other industries, perhaps trying to emulate its past glories which are attested by both the thousands of ancient workshops and galleries, and the industrial buildings from the past two centuries, not to mention the old neoclassical buildings. This coexistence of so many industrial periods, prompted the National Technical School, in cooperation with the European Union and other agencies, to begin creating a Technological - Cultural Park in the area of the former French Association.

Also worthy of note is the Mineralogical Museum, unique in Greece, and housed in a restored building, which contains most of the known minerals of Lavriotiki.

Next to Lavrio is ancient Thorikos with perhaps the oldest theater in Attica, the Arma of Thespis, in an unusual ellipsoidal shape.

Left: Sounion.   Below: Lavrio, the town that stads as a monument to ancient and modern industrlial technology and architecture.

13
EASTERN
& WESTERN ATTICA

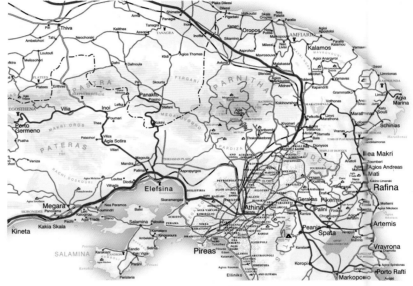

For most everyone Attica is the place where Greek civilization accomplished great things, the place that nourished Athens. However, Attica is so rich in history, sites, and multiformity, that its unknown features can only be the result of the blinding light cast by Athens. In and around the Attic basin are areas whose history and beauty are equal of Athens itself. Leaving the capital to the east one comes upon beautiful suburbs such as **Spata, Paiania and Markopoulo**. On the shores of this area are to be found **Porto Rafti**, the coast of Artemis, and the important archaeological site at **Brauron with the temple of Artemis.** To the north are **Pallini** and **Pikermi** where in the 19th century were discovered a treasure of Paleontological finds, 13 million years old. High up, on the back part of Penteli is the small monastery of **Tao-Pentelis**. You encounter the sea once more at Rafina the most important harbor in Attica after Piraeus. Heading north along the coast you will come upon a number of resorts such as **Mati, Ayios Andreas,** and **Nea Makri** where a large number of Athenians gather in the summer.

Then comes **Marathon** one of the most important places in the history of Greece and Europe where in 490 B.C. the Athenians stopped the advance of the Persians to the north. Near Marathon lies **Rhamnous**, a continuation of the ancient deme of the same name and then **Amphiareion** an archaeological site on an especially beautiful site. West of Athens you will reach Eleusis, in an industrial region of the Thriasian Plain.

Here was once of the most important sanctuaries in antiquity where Demeter was worshipped and the famous "Eleusinian Mysteries" were conducted. Further west lies **Megara**, also an ancient deme and one of the most powerful.

The Mesogeia: *The district that lies behind Hymettus and starts at Stavros and goes all the way to Lavrio. It is identified with wine and resin.*

Spata - Artemis - Brauron

Spata *(20 km.) is one of the most famous villages in the Mesogeia. During the grape harvest in September the sight to see is the grapes being turned into must. The new airport of Athens (Eleftherios Venizelos) is being built at Spata. After Spata comes the large beach at Artemis which to the left goes all the way to Rafina and right is a continuation of Brauron along the shore.* **Brauron** *is the homeland of the Peisistratos clan, of Miltiadis and Kimon. The sanctuary of Artemis Brauronia was founded to the back of the bay and at the foot of the hill with a fortified prehistoric acropolis; it was one of the most ancient and respected temples in Attica. Artemis Brauronia was worshipped*

The area around Artemida.

The goddess Artemis of Braurona (Brauron Museum).

as the goddess of vegetation, the protectress of fruits and animals, and the goddess of the hunt and the outdoor life. At the same time she was the protectress of women, particularly at the critical time of childbirth. The goddess was served by maidens 5-10 years old, the Arktoi ("Bears"), who during festivals, danced in their yellow attire like bears, the animals sacred to the goddess. Excavations have brought to light the temple of Artemis. In a **local museum** *are housed reliefs with representations of the worship of the goddess.*

Paiania - Markopoulo

To the right of Stavros lies **Paiania**, *one of the oldest demes of Attica, the homeland of the great politician and orator of antiquity, Demosthenes. The* **Vorres Museum** *is in the area while the ascent up the slopes of Mt. Hymettus takes you to the* **Koutouki Cave**. *The cave is four km. from Paiania and a twisting road ends on a edge that is like a balcony facing the Mesogeia.*
The incredible stalactite and stalagmite formations, with their mythical names, lend an air of phantasmagoria to this cave.
After Paiania, comes **Markopoulo** *which is renowned for its vineyards and its excellent wine. Right of Markopoulo is* **Koropi** *and left the road goes to* **Porto Rafti**.

Porto Rafti (Mesogea Harbor)

Porto Rafti, *a bustling summer resort, is built in a small idyllic bay south of Brauron. It is identified with the ancient deme of Prassies. Prassies was an important harbor in Attica. From here sailed the ships of the official Athenian "Theoria" (Mission) to the celebrations of Apollo on Delos. Pausanias says: From Markopoulo you reach Lavrio going through Keratea and Thorikos (page 141).*

Pikermi

From Stavros the road to Marathon reaches Pikermi after going through **Pallini**. Here during the 19th century a large paleontological treasure consisting of fossilized skeletons of dinosaurs, who had lived in what is now Greece 13 million years ago, was discovered, found to the rear of a natural ravine. Thousands of animals: mastodons, rhinoceri, lions, apes, and Mediterranean ponies were found at the back of that ravine obviously driven there by a great fire. These fossils are on exhibit at the **Paleontological Museum** of the University of Athens.

On the back side of Mt. Penteli and above the village of Pikermi is the small church and monastery of **Tao-Pentelis.** ("Daou Pentelis", 16th century). The original monastery was destroyed at the end of the 10th century by invaders. The monastery contains ancient and Byzantine sculpture and inscriptions.

Rafina

Rafina lies to the right of Pikermi (26 km.). It is one of the oldest harbors of Attica and serves a large number of the Cycladic islands with a regular schedule of ferry boats.

Mati - Ayios Andreas - Nea Makri

Continuing along Marathonos Avenue you reach Mati, a verdant seaside area and then **Ayios Andreas** (30 km.). The pine trees come right down to the sea. At Ayios Andreas there is an organized campsite. This is followed by **Nea Makri** (31 km.) another summer resort area. From here a road left goes up the slopes of Mt. Pentelis. At the site of Ayios Petros, where there is an exceptional view of the Gulf of Euboea, two roads lead to the city of Athens.

Rafina,
the second largest port in Attica.

Marathon

After Nea Makri a turn-off to the right takes you to **Tymvos, Marathon** and its **Museum**. In 490 B.C. there was a famous battle on the **plain of Marathon**.
The 192 Athenians who were killed in the battle were buried in the mound of Tymvos which is 12 m. high and has a circumference of 185 m. From the spot of the battle, which is 42 km. from Athens, the first Marathon runner set off to bring the joyful message to Athens. "We won" he said and then dropped dead.
This is also the point where the modern **Marathon Race** (also 42 km.) begins.If you continue on the road past Tymvos you will pass through the village of **Marathonas** and end up at the Marathon dam. You can also get there from Athens on a shorter road going past Kifissia, Ayios Stephanos, and then to the dam (31 km).
You can make excursions with a view of the lake through the elegant areas around **Lake Marathonas**.

Above: The "Ephebe of Marathon" (The Archaeological Museum of Athens).

Below: The burial mound for those who died at the Battle of Maratho, erected by the Athenians in 490 B.C.

Rhamnous

From the village of Marathonas the road goes to **Kato Souli** and **Rhamnous** after passing through **Schoinia**. Rhamnous lies at the end of the northwest coast of Attica, after **Ayia Marina**. The ancient deme of Rhamnous was here as well as one of the most important sanctuaries in Attica, dedicated to Nemesis, which flourished during the 4th century B.C. The sanctuary of Nemesis (Divine Justice) was built at the beginning of the 5th century B.C. on the top of a hill. In the nave of the temple the statues of Themis, a priestess of Nemesis, Arsinoe, and Lysikleidis were found.

The statue of Nemesis, a work of the Parian sculptor Agorakritos, a student of Phidias, was erected in the flagged nave of the temple. Pausanias has described the statue of Nemesis in detail. The fortification of Rhamnous protected the town as well as the entrance to Evripos.

Behind the stoa was a small theater that could hold 3,000. The ruins of the Roman baths were found beyond all that.
On the opposite side of the ravine, the excavations have brought to light the ruins of inns, that also served for therapy, and a clepsydra. Amphiaraos, in whose honor this oracular complex was built, was himself a seer.
He came to a tragic end. He disappeared with his chariot into a chasm in the earth, wounded by Zeus. Later Zeus repented and made him immortal.
There is an interesting museum at the site of the antiquities. At the end of September there was a celebration in honor of Amphiaraos at the Amphiareion.
An all night vigil was held there, followed by a procession, a sacrifice and finally contests.

Amphiareion

Amphiareion is another of the archaeological sites in Attica unique for its beauty; it is 45 km. from Athens, in the area of Kalamos. The sanctuary there, a large Archaic structure, is dedicated to one of the Seven Against Thebes, the hero from Argos, Amphiarios. His sanctuary lies near a spring with medicinal water and was a combination of an oracle and a place for healing and was built in the Doric style in the 4th century B.C. The temple, that lay in a ravine, also contained a large altar. Everyone who went there wanted advice from the oracle. Near the altar was a sacred fountain. Its water from drunk by pilgrims out of large shells - a few of these were found in the excavations. In addition, a very large room was discovered with 30 bases for statues all set in a row and a large gallery - the Incubation Portico as it was called - where the patients were sent to sleep after their therapy, to wait for a prophetic dream.

The hero and healer Amphiaraos.
Detail from a commemorative relief (5th century B.C.,
The Archaeological Museum of Athens).

Eleusis

Eleusis is 22 kilometers west of Athens on a plain known as the Thriasian Plain on the road that goes to the Peloponnese and mainland Greece. Today it is an industrial town. In antiquity Eleusis was one of the most important sanctuaries, dedicated to the worship of Demeter and her daughter Persephone, and connected to the Eleusinian Mysteries and the succession of the seasons.

The myth says that while playing one day in a flowering meadow with the Oceanids, Persephone (or Kore as she was called), the daughter of Demeter and Zeus, was abducted by Pluto the King of Hades who came up through a chasm in the earth and took her down to his dark kingdom, the land of the dead. Inconsolable, her mother wandered for nine months between the sky and the earth searching with lighted torches for traces of her lost daughter until learning from the all knowing Sun (Ilios) what had occurred, renounced Olympus and went into human towns disguised as an old woman. Arriving at Eleusis she received the hospitality of the local king, Keleos. She undertook the raising of the little Demophontas who she secretly placed in the fire every night to insure his immortality. When Metaneira, the mother of Demophontas, found out, she was forced to reveal her identity and commanded Keleos to build a large temple and altar under the Acropolis. There the goddess Demeter locked herself up in anger which caused a drought and terrible famine over the whole earth. Then Zeus was forced to bring Persephone back to earth. In the future, Zeus decreed, Persephone would spend two-thirds of the year with her mother and the other third in the Kingdom of Hades. These periods of time symbolized the changes of the seasons of the year and the periodicity of the farming cycle. Before she left Eleusis for Olympus Demeter taught Keleos the Eleusinian Mysteries and declared that they should be remain inviolate and secret. The systematic cultivation of the earth was also established at that time.

The **Eleusinian Mysteries** became a form of universal worship during the Roman period. There are countless theories which have tried to interpret the mysteries. Unlike elsewhere in Greece, where religion was open to all, at Eleusis the Mysteries were controlled by a small, closed group of initiates who had sworn to uphold the strict confidentiality of the secret rites. During the time of Solon (600 B.C.) Eleusis was annexed to Athens. In a short while the Mysteries became Panhellenic.

The archaeological finds show the great development of the site. In 480 B.C. the Persians left Eleusis in ruins. The Mysteries have also been connected to the activities of Kimon, Pericles, Iktinos, and Lykourgos to name but a few. The appearance of Christianity led to the decline of the Eleusinian religion.

Views of the archaeological site at Eleusis.

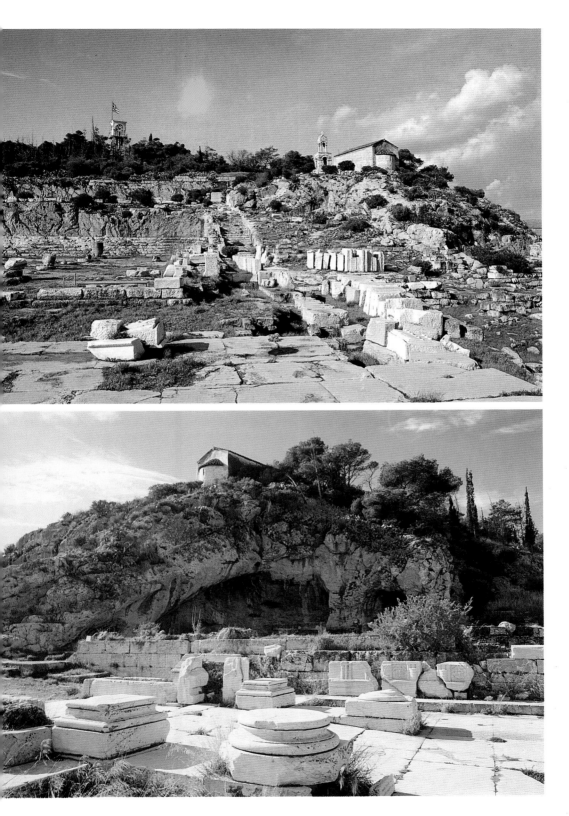

The persecutions of the Byzantine emperor Theodosius, who forbade the ancient religion, and the invasion of Alaric in 395 B.C. destroyed a part of the sanctuary while the attacks of the early Christians reduced the renowned temple to ruins. **The archaeological site at Eleusis** is one of the richest in Greece. It starts at the external yard where the Sacred Way from Athens ended; this is followed by large porticoes, a rectangular fountain, arches, public and private buildings from Roman times, hot springs, inns and baths for the pilgrims. In the center of the yard is the amphiprostyle of the temple of the propylaia of Artemis and Poseidon, the Kalichoros Frear (the ancient well) where women danced in honor of Demeter and Persephone. The Greater Propylaia is followed by the sanctuary, the Roman Prytaneum, the sacred dwelling of Kirykos, and the underground cisterns. The Romans built the Small Propylaia of pendelic marble. From there you enter the main temple space. There is found the Plutonion, the temple of Pluto Hades, and in the cavity of the rock, the chasm through which the god of the underworld led Persephone back to earth. The internal Sacred Way takes you to wide stairs. The nearly amphitheatrical formation of the space leads to the hypothesis that the mysteries were held there. Continuing along the Sacred Way you reach the famous Eleusinian Telesterio. The god no longer lives there nor in any of the other ancient Greek telesteria. It held 3,000 spectators of the Mysteries. The Palace was in the center of the hall of the Telesterion.

The Museum of Eleusis is at the archaeological site. In it are found noteworthy displays of Archaic, Classical, Hellenistic and Roman sculpture, as well as ceramics, weapons, copper and gold jewellery from the prehistoric period. In addition, there are pots and dedications, a headless statue of Demeter, a work by the Parian sculptor Agorakritos, and the marvelous Proto-Attican amphora with depictions of the blinding of Polyphemus by Odysseus.

Megara

After Eleusis the road heads on toward Corinth passing through The Megarid. At the beginning of the first millennium B.C. The Megarid was inhabited by the Dorians and was united into a powerful state with its center at Megara.

Euclid, a disciple of Socrates, founded the famed Megaran School of Philosophy (440-380 B.C.). In 146 B.C. it was subjugated by Rome. During certain times in history this district has been an independent state with its capital at Megara. In the archaeological collection at Megara are pieces of sculpture from Classical and Roman times as well as ceramics from all periods. The old automobile road Megara-Corinth passes along an area that falls straight to the sea, which is dangerous and picturesque at the same time; this is **Kakia Skala**. Many myths and stories are connected to the area, beginning in mythological times. Here were also the **Scironian Rocks**; Sciron stood at the top of them and threw passersby into the sea. The area was delivered when Theseus, the hero of Athens, killed Sciron in the same way.

Kineta is the final coastal spot in Attica. It is a pretty town with houses and gardens which go down to the sea.

Finds from Eleusis.
Above: Marble relief of Demeter and Persephone.

Below: Black-figured depiction of the blinding of Polyphemus by Odysseus.

From Eleusis to Panakto

Leaving Eleusis, and following the old National Road you go to the fortress of **Oinoe**, the present-day Mazi (21 km. from Thebes). On the right side of the road there is an ancient tower where torches were placed for the transmission of messages by fire. The ancient ruins of Oinoe to the northeast consist of the tower and walls from the 5th and 4th century B.C. Continuing along the road toward Thebes from Eleusis (the old National Road) you enter the area of ancient Elefthera Oinoe. The road to the left after Oinoe goes to the village of **Villia** (54 km. from Athens). This is a pretty and delightfully cool village on the slopes of Mt. Kithaironas. The enchanting site of **Elateia** is at an altitude of 1,400 m. 18 kilometers after Villia comes **Porto Germeno**, the ancient **Aigosthena**. The ancient town of Aigosthena lies approximately in the middle of the gulf. The ancient seer and healer Melabous was worshipped here. The acropolis of Aigosthena had eight towers and two gates. The fortifications are from the 4th century B.C. Today Aigosthena, or Porto Germeno, is a summer resort settlement. The road after Oinoe passes through the narrows of Kaza and reaches **Eleftheres**. The inhabitants of ancient Eleftheres joined together in the 6th century B.C. with Attica and brought to Athens the worship of Dionysos. The famous sculptor in bronze Myron was also from Eleftheres; his statue, the "Discus-Thrower" ("Discobolus"), has immortalized the moment of the athlete's supreme endeavor. At the entrance to the narrows which connect Attica to Boeotia is the large **Panakto** fortification situated on the border. It was built in the 4th century B.C. It consisted of square two-storey towers. Seven gates can be discerned as well as the ruins of a military encampment.

14

THE SARONIC GULF

Salamis - Aegina - Poros - Hydra - Spetses

The Saronic Gulf, that captivating gulf of Attica, and containing islands of a variety of size, is a priceless gem. Athenians are fortunate to be able to reach these islands in a short time and get far from the hustle and bustle of the city. The nearest one of them is historic Salamis which is also the most densely populated. Leaving Perama in Attica, in a quarter of an hour you find yourself at Paloukia and from there you can go wherever you want by car. Further south is beautiful Aegina, with its pine groves, sand beaches and the renowned temple of Afaia which is only one hour from Piraeus by boat. It is also heavily populated but not as heavily as Salamis. Even further south is picturesque Poros, opposite the shores of the Peloponnese, and still further famous Hydra with its traditional architecture. Finally, just a bit further south, at the entrance to the Gulf of Argos, lies Spetses, pic-turesque and verdant. With a naval tradition as long as that of Hydra it played with its fleet and experienced sailors a crucial role in the uprising of the nation against the Turks in 1821.No more than four hours separate Spetses, the furthest island, from Piraeus by boat. But if this journey is made with the swift "Flying Dolphin" hydrofoils that have schedules to all these islands (except Salamis) then the time is cut in half. Besides the five main islands there are also smaller ones which come to more than 100 if you count the rocky outcroppings. Of these only 11 are inhabited. Those that are uninhabited may provide you with pleasant surprizes if you visit them with your own boat.So an opportunity for an unforgettable trip from Athens, be it for one day or many, is provided by the islands of the Saronic Gulf and the Gulf of Argos which for the sake of brevity is usually called the Argosaronic Gulf.

The picturesque town of Hydra with its famed stone houses and beautifl harbor.

Salamis

This is the largest island in the Saronic Gulf and the closest to Athens. The island is covered with pine and has beautiful beaches along its south coast. You can go to Salamis on small boats from Piraeus and by ferry boat from Perama, at Paloukia, and from Perama Megara at Fane-romeni. Salamis is known as the island of Aias, Homer's hero who lead the Salaminians during the Trojan War. But above all else it is known for the famous naval battle that was fought in its straits in 480 B.C. between the Persian and Athenian fleets. The Athenians won and were thus saved from this terrible threat for once and for all.

Aegina

The second largest of the islands, Aegina lies in the middle of the Saronic Gulf, with an area of 85 sq. km. and a coastline of 57 km. Its more than 11,000 permanent inhabitants are primarily involved with the cultivation of pistachio nuts. The Aegina pistachio is renowned and is the island's main product. Aegina is 16 nautical miles from Piraeus and the journey by ferry boat takes only

A charming little church on the harbor of Aegina

one hour, while the Flying Dolphin hydrofoils cut the time in half. According to mythology the first king of the island was the hero Aiakos, the son of Zeus and the Nymph Aegina. Aegina is an island full of life, that has retained its color and picturesqueness. In the port of Aegina one can visit the Archaeological Museum, at Kolona (Column), all that is left of the ancient temple of Apollo located next to the harbor, and the Cathedral and the first Government House of modern Greece.Eleven kilometers east of the harbor and the capital of Aegina, is the **temple of Afaia**, an ancient goddess and protectress of the island,

The ancient Temple of Afaia Athena on Aegina.

perched on top of a hill. The temple is in a Doric style and was built after the naval victory at Salamis on an idyllic site with a view of the sea and the coasts of Attica opposite. This excursion ends at the beautiful sand beach of Ayia Marina. There are also sand beaches with good swimming on the north shores of the island (Souvala and Vaia) and on the west shores too where the road ends at the quaint fishing village of Perdika, opposite the pine-covered islet of **Moni**.

In the interior of the island, on the way to the temple of Afaia, is **Palaiochora**, a deserted medieval village and the **Convent of Ayios Nektarios** which celebrates on 9 November. The village of Pacheia Rachi is found on the slopes of Mt. Oros (531 m.), the highest mountain on the island, at the summit of which are traces of the ruins of a sanctuary to Ellanios Zeus. At a distance of 3 nautical miles west of Aegina is the lush and verdant island of **Angistri** with its crystal-clear water and picturesque settlements. It has daily connections with Piraeus and Aegina.

Poros

The word Poros means passage in Greek. And it is also a fitting name for this island. It lies in the southwest part of the Saronic Gulf opposite the Argolid in the Peloponnese. At the end of this passage is an island town that strikes one as cheerful, and it is built amphitheatrically on a hill. This is the harbor of Poros and the main settlement on the island. Opposite, only ten minutes by small boat, are the dark green shores of the Peloponnese at Galatas, with its renowned lemon grove. The island has daily connections with Piraeus (31 nautical miles). Half an hour from the harbor, on a hill, is found the sanctuary of Poseidon which was the center of the oldest naval amphictyony (7th century B.C.).

Near the temple was the ancient town of Kalavria. West of the harbor is Neorio with beautiful sand beaches and pine trees. To the east is the coastal settlement of Askeli. Further east there is a view of the lemon grove and the convent of Zoodochos Pigi founded in the 16th century.

The lovely town of Poros.

Hydra

A marvelous little cosmopolitan town juts out before you as the ship turns and enters the harbor of Hydra. It is three hours from Piraeus by ship and 1.30 hours by hydrofoil (37 nautical miles). Hydra is a picturesque Saronic Gulf island known since antiquity and which has a glorious history.

Around the harbor of Hydra stand the old mansions of the captains, nobles and admirals from the period both before and after the Greek War of Independence of 1821. The Merchant Marine School occupies one of them and another houses an annex of the School of Fine Arts of the Athens National Technical School.

At the entrance to the harbor there still can be seen the old cannons that guarded the town. In the middle of the waterfront is the monastery of the Koimisis tis Theotokou (The Dormition of the Virgin), the present-day cathedral of Hydra. It is worth winding your way up through the narrow lanes to the top of the hills.

From there you can admire the view of the harbor and at the same time enjoy a splendid sunset. A marvelous view is also afforded by the ascent to the monastery of Profitis Ilias (Prophet Elijah), located in the center of the island at an altitude of 500 meters.

Those who like the sea can swim in the deep waters of Spilia, which is next to the harbor, at the beach of Mandraki with its organized facilities, at Kaminia with its large pebbles and at Vlycho. There are more distant beaches at Molos and Bisti. No automobiles are allowed on Hydra so caiques are the only way to reach the beaches on the island.

View of the harbor of Hydra.

Spetses

Spetses is not a part of the Saronic Gulf but we are describing it because it forms a unit with the other islands. Covered with pine groves it lies at the entrance to the Gulf of Argos and has a lively night life. Automobiles are forbidden on this island as well. You can get to Spetses from Piraeus (52 nautical miles) or from Kosta in the Peloponnese. Spetses, the capital of the island, is on the NE coast, opposite Kosta (10 minutes by small boat). Dapia square in front of the harbor is impressive. One can still find there, next to the little cafe tables, the cannons that were used during the Greek War of Independence of 1821. The museum and a few old mansions remind one of the island's former glory and wealth. Besides the beaches near the harbor, Spetses also has other beautiful beaches and idyllic bays. South of Spetses is the lush green, private island of Spetsopoula.

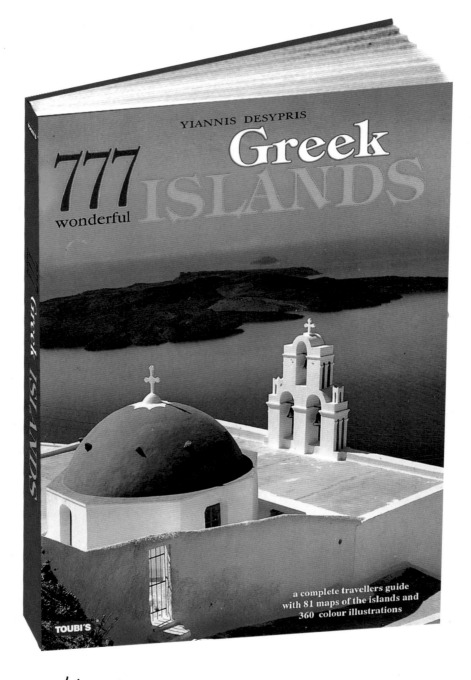

YIANNIS DESYPRIS

777 wonderful Greek ISLANDS

a complete travellers guide
with 81 maps of the islands and
360 colour illustrations

TOUBI'S

$\mathcal{M}$any years in preparation, now completed in 1994.
A unique edition which treats 777 beautiful Greek Islands
from the 9,500 islands and rocky outcroppings of the
Greek Archipelago.
360 colour illustrations, 81 maps of the islands,
format: 17 × 24, pages: 272